"This book holds information and advice that could easily save many a dancer's career. It's written with a clarity and compassion that come from a woman who knows first-hand both the difficulties and the thrilling joys of being a dancer."
  —Bebe Neuwirth, Emmy and Tony Award–winning Broadway dancer, singer, and actress, and founder of the Dancers' Resource at the Actors Fund

"*The Dancer's Way* is full of important and interesting information. I am impressed with its accessibility and practical applicability, not only for dancers, but also for medical doctors and all other health-care providers involved in the care of dancers. With this comprehensive book, Linda Hamilton places herself in the forefront of dance medicine in its broadest sense. The book breathes the passion of a dancer and the skills of a writer, combined with the professionalism of the psychologist she is now. Highly recommended, a joy to read, and, although dedicated to dancers, a 'must' for everyone active or interested in dance and/or dance medicine. Thank you, Linda, for sharing with us your vast knowledge and experience in two beautiful worlds, of dance and academia."
  —A. B. M. (Boni) Rietveld, M.D., president of the International Association for Dance Medicine & Science

"If you're serious about a career in dance or just want to move through the rest of your life with grace, Linda Hamilton choreographs a perfect path. *The Dancer's Way* is the complete companion for anyone who wants the body, mind, and spirit of a dancer— a true athlete. I think I will make it required reading for all of my Broadway Gypsies. Thank you, Linda, for taking the time to share these important truths for making the most of and maintaining the dancer's physical gift."
  —Jerry Mitchell, Tony Award winner, director and choreographer of *Legally Blonde: The Musical,* and mentor of Bravo's reality competition *Step It Up and Dance*

"Yummy book. It's the 'fit' dancers have been waiting for. *Eat fit, work fit, feel fit, live fit, dance fit.*"
  —Grover Dale, Tony Award–winning director and founder of Answers4Dancers.com

"Meticulously researched and written with a warm and generous tone, Linda Hamilton's *The Dancer's Way* is an invaluable guide for dancers of any age."
  —Meredith Monk, *Dance Magazine* and MacArthur Genius Award–winning composer and choreographer

"Linda Hamilton has lived this book. I've followed her career since she was in New York City Ballet and took my classes. She has become such a wise and understanding person who truly knows how difficult it is to be a dancer today and keep your sanity. This book is especially important for young dancers because it is a treasure chest of new information that can eliminate pain, doubt, and fear. Brava!"
  —Finis Jhung, former principal dancer at Harkness Ballet and master ballet teacher

Also by Linda H. Hamilton, Ph.D.

Advice for Dancers: Emotional Counsel and Practical Strategies
The Person Behind the Mask: A Guide to Performing Arts Psychology

The Dancer's Way

The New York City Ballet Guide to
Mind, Body, and Nutrition

LINDA H. HAMILTON, Ph.D., and
New York City Ballet

Foreword by PETER MARTINS,
Ballet Master in Chief, New York City Ballet

Photography by PAUL KOLNIK

ST. MARTIN'S GRIFFIN ☙ New York

Neither the publisher nor the author is engaged in rendering medical advice or services to the individual reader. The ideas, procedures, and suggestions contained in this book are not intended as a substitute for consulting with your physician. Neither the author nor the publisher shall be liable or responsible for any loss or damage allegedly arising from any information or suggestion in this book.

www.stmartins.com

Book design by Gretchen Achilles

Photo on page ii: NYCB dancers in Jerome Robbins's *Glass Pieces*. Cover photo: Wendy Whelan and Albert Evans in Christopher Wheeldon's *Liturgy*.

LIBRARY OF CONGRESS CATALOGING-IN-PUBLICATION DATA

Hamilton, Linda H.
    The dancer's way : the New York City Ballet guide to mind, body, and nutrition / Linda H. Hamilton.—1st ed.
        p.   cm.
Includes bibliographical references and index.
    ISBN-13: 978-0-312-34235-7
    ISBN-10: 0-312-34235-7
    1. Ballet—Study and teaching—New York (State)—New York.
2. Ballet dancers—New York (State)—New York.   3. Ballet—
Vocational guidance.   I. New York City Ballet.   II. Title.
    GV1788.5.H36 2009
    792.807—dc22

                                                    2008030150

10   9   8   7   6   5   4   3   2

To all dancers who want to reach their full potential without compromising their health or careers

Contents

Acknowledgments

I am indebted to the dancers who so generously shared their time and personal insights with me, with special thanks to New York City Ballet (NYCB) members Megan LeCrone and Abi Stafford, whom I followed in our wellness program throughout their recovery from injuries. Your voices, more than anything else, put a human face to *The Dancer's Way*. I am also deeply grateful to NYCB's core medical team for their invaluable input and to the company's artistic and administrative staff for their assistance, with gratitude to Ken Tabachnick for his thorough review of the manuscript, Ellen Sorrin for her thoughtful comments on food preparation, and Peter Martins for having the vision to make our wellness program possible. Other dance medicine specialists who deserve recognition include Phillip Bauman (orthopedist), Hilary Cartwright (Gyrotonic and yoga instructor), Katy Keller (physical therapist), Deanne Lay (Pilates instructor), Thomas Novella (podiatrist), Laura Pumillo (registered dietician), Heidi Skolnik (certified dietician), Michelle Warren (endocrinologist), and Mathew Wyon (exercise physiologist). This handbook would never have existed in its current form without the cogent feedback from my editors at St. Martin's Press, Sheila Curry Oakes and Alyse Diamond, *Dance Magazine* editors Hanna Rubin and Wendy Perron, and my agent, Al Zuckerman at Writers House. On a more personal note, I am most thankful for the unwavering love and support of my husband, Dr. William Hamilton, and my mother, Helen Homek.

Foreword

Dancers' lives are centered around their bodies. Throughout their careers, they face the difficult challenge of remaining slender and graceful while maintaining exceptional strength and flexibility. When watching them perform, one forgets that these elegant beings who bring beauty to the world's stages with seemingly effortless leaps and lifts are continually faced with the same physical demands as world-class athletes.

I have been very fortunate to have had the opportunity to participate in the evolution of New York City Ballet, and my involvement has enabled me to reflect on the fundamental role our bodies have played in our history. When George Balanchine founded the company in 1948, he revolutionized ballet. Balanchine fused traditional classical vocabulary with modern concepts to create mysterious and striking combinations, and dancers' bodies were the ideal medium for his neoclassical language. Under his leadership and artistic direction, steps and movements became heightened, quickened, and extended.

While Balanchine's transformations enriched the dance world and attracted a wider audience, they also placed greater demands on his dancers' bodies. He acknowledged the athletic aspects of dance by hiring a company physical therapist and orthopedist. Today we have had to adjust to the even larger demands that are being placed on NYCB dancers. Balanchine's ballets are being performed by dancers who jump higher, move with greater agility, and dance with greater versatility than those a generation ago. Furthermore, our repertory of over 150 ballets is continuing to grow and expand in its diversity. In the same season, our dancers can be expected to perform Balanchine's neoclassical movements, a Broadway-influenced ballet by Jerome Robbins, and new works by contemporary choreographers. In response to this increased versatility and the growing desire for constant renewal through innovative forms of choreography, a new emphasis has been placed on decreasing the stress on different parts of the body that accompanies the adaptation to diverse technical styles.

Our wellness program was founded in 2001 to respond to the rising awareness of the physical demands of ballet. The goal has been to cultivate our dancers' health and performance potential by supplementing medical treatment with the knowledge necessary to prevent injury. The program's health-care professionals consist of psychologist Linda Hamilton, orthopedist William Hamilton, physical therapist Marika Molnar, chiropractor Lawrence DeMann, Jr., and nutritionist Joy Bauer. Since the program's inception, the company's workers' compensation claims and disability have been reduced. Our dancers are now more aware of the consequences of unhealthy behaviors, such as lack of sleep or a poor diet. They also possess a greater understanding of their bodies, recognize the benefits of cross-conditioning, and are committed to increasing their energy levels and optimizing performance.

Although ballet requires more training than a high-level contact sport, its athleticism will always be overshadowed by its artistry. Ballet dancers have reached a keen understanding of this reality. Not only are our dancers committed to achieving technical precision, but they are dedicated to making their movements look effortless. They are conscious of the beautiful illusions they create and seek to inspire audiences through their art.

The Dancer's Way highlights the techniques and strategies advanced by the NYCB wellness program; however, anyone with an interest in self-improvement can learn from the struggles and achievements of our dancers. This guide reveals the extraordinary preparation behind the mysterious arrangements that we see onstage. Our dancers today are remarkably self-aware. Their commitment drives them to understand their bodies, acknowledge their vulnerabilities, and respond effectively to the physical demands of the dance world. Yet this awareness extends beyond themselves—when I observe them working toward improvement and navigating change, I see them glow with confidence.

I am extremely grateful to Linda Hamilton and the other dedicated and talented members of our medical team, and I thank them for their ongoing commitment to enhancing the health and strength of our dancers. As the dance world evolves, our wellness program will continue to prove that the more we learn, the more we can achieve.

—PETER MARTINS
Ballet Master in Chief
New York City Ballet

Introduction

First and foremost, I want you to know that we care—about you, your hopes, and your dreams. Although *The Dancer's Way* is directed toward the 11 million people engaged in some form of dance in the United States, anyone with an interest in fitness can benefit from our holistic approach to exercise. The book *New York City Ballet Workout* by Peter Martins and New York City Ballet, with Howard Kaplan, showed readers how to build leanness and flexibility in the muscles and limbs through the magic of ballet. This guide takes you to the next level to achieve peak performance by sharing the secrets of dancers in one of the world's greatest companies.

Peter Martins, Ballet Master in Chief of New York City Ballet, opened the door to our wellness program in 2001, based on research I conducted with my colleagues, William G. Hamilton, M.D., Marika Molnar, P.T., and Lawrence DeMann, Jr., D.C. We designed the program to help dancers reach their potential without compromising their health, with annual screenings, educational seminars, cooking classes, and individual counseling. Traditionally, dancers and companies focus on technique, treating problems after they occur. Now we recognize that the beneficial aspects of dancing can be undermined by risk factors such as constant stress, sleep deprivation, and poor nutrition. What makes our approach so special is that in only three years, it has cut disability in NYCB by 46 percent, impressive considering that ballet is more physically and mentally demanding than professional football.

My contribution as the company's wellness consultant involves helping dancers cope with occupational stress. I should know. Being a former dancer who dropped out of high school to join NYCB, I learned the hard way, after enduring multiple sprained ankles, a bad back, and "jumper's knee," that overworking was my downfall. Dancers have a great work ethic, but, like many high achievers, we often feel uncomfortable with the idea of pacing ourselves or being patient enough to completely rehabilitate an injury. Instead, we do more classes, more exercises, and, often, more damage. After my fourth sprained ankle, I realized that dancers and other practicing athletes needed reliable information to help avoid injuries. No matter how you slice it, there is no way to achieve your goals on crutches.

My decision to help myself and others had several effects. First, I was able to recover from my current injury by doing Pilates before returning to dance class. This exercise program helped me overcome my usual impatience with being unable to dance and kept me safer from serious injuries by helping me maintain my overall strength and flexibility. I also decided to pursue higher education—but first I had to pass my high school equivalency test. My goal was to become a psychologist who specialized in the performing arts. Peter Martins played a significant role in making this dream come true by allowing me to attend school full-time for eight years while performing. My primary responsibility through it all was to stay in shape as a dancer.

Since receiving my doctorate in clinical and research psychology, I have done extensive epidemiological studies on occupational stress in dancers from America, Europe, China, and Russia, in addition to consulting with dancers in my private practice. I have also sought to reduce work-related problems through my monthly advice column in *Dance Magazine,* which I've been writing since 1992. I have written two books and more than fifty articles on topics as varied as weight management and performance anxiety. These experiences, combined with my own as a performer, have made me acutely aware of the challenges and needs of dancers.

I wrote this book to help serious dancers maintain a healthy mind and body while performing, based on what we have learned at NYCB's wellness program. While many readers may consider highly trained professionals to be out of their league, everyone can benefit from our program's scientific principles, which have been refined to meet the needs of dancers of varying ages, styles, and fitness levels. This guide is geared primarily to female dance students and professionals eighteen to thirty-eight years old, with special tips for youngsters.

In Part 1 of this book, I outline the challenges in dance, and how our wellness program can help you achieve your goals by establishing a healthy lifestyle and navigating the road to change.

In Part 2 readers will learn ways to avoid common roadblocks to fitness, including stress, burnout, injuries, and eating problems, with our five keys to peak performance:

1. Good work habits

2. Cross-training activities

3. Eating right to stay fit

4. Effective weight control strategies

5. Stress management techniques

Understanding how the five keys affect performance will be critical to your success. Many dancers struggle with a no pain, no gain attitude, and they tend to ignore chronic signs of hunger or fatigue. Others demand perfection without making allowances for growth spurts, mistakes, or minor anatomical differences, such as unequal turnout. While it is common for high achievers to go for the gold at the expense of their health, lack of information can result in a serious injury. In extreme cases, it can mean the end of a promising career. This book provides crucial insights into each key, how it is helpful, and the various options that are especially effective for dancers.

Part 3 includes a number of useful resources, and describes in detail several beneficial annual screenings, which you can duplicate with a dance medicine specialist. A final component involves the use of diaries to modify food intake and emotional stress.

Interviews with NYCB performers and dance medicine specialists are included throughout the book. Readers will follow two injured members of the company, Abi Stafford and Megan LeCrone, as they recover and are able to return to the stage. There are also composites of clients from my private practice to illustrate the concerns of dancers outside the company; in these cases, the names and identifying characteristics have been changed to preserve anonymity.

My job is to help dancers develop a healthy approach to fitness by offering advice, removing barriers, and clarifying goals at each step of the way. In this book, I offer you the same heartfelt guidance. Change is scary, but it provides a unique opportunity to learn, to grow, and to hope for a brighter future—as a dancer and as a person!

PART ONE

Opening the Door to Peak Performance

ONE

New York City Ballet's Wellness Program

I've had to acquire athleticism like strength and stamina—not just artistry—to get through the hardest repertoire today!

—ASHLEY BOUDER, NYCB principal

New York City Ballet cofounder George Balanchine likened his dancers to thoroughbred racehorses. Dance aficionados may scoff at the comparison, but there is no denying the athletic aspects of this constantly evolving art form. Extreme dance, multiple techniques, and acrobatic moves—all are par for the course in the current dance scene. The dilemma for aspiring professionals is that dance classes no longer prepare you to perform at this level. But do not despair! This book provides you with a concrete plan to reach your potential, based on NYCB's proven wellness program for serious dancers.

How can our program help you achieve your goals? Unlike in the past, when dancing longer and harder was the only way to excel, now there are practical tools to overcome common challenges, including physical and mental stress. NYCB principal dancer Jenifer Ringer agrees with Ashley Bouder that being an athlete is essential, after multiple injuries almost ended her promising career. "I'm so excited about the wellness program," she says. "It's incredible what you're doing for dancers."

You, too, can benefit by using New York City Ballet's program, which we have tailored to meet the needs of all dancers, not just in ballet. To begin, let's take a look at what it means to be a dancer in the twenty-first century.

LEFT (Ashley Bouder in Jerome Robbins's *The Four Seasons*)

Dancing in the New Millennium

Previous generations of dancers focused on a specific technique to succeed as a performer. Today's dancers do not have this luxury. Instead, they face unique requirements, and chief among them is the need to perform in vastly different genres. This new focus on versatility is both exciting and challenging. On the positive side, mastering more than one dance technique definitely expands your prospects for finding employment. The downside is that it stresses different areas of the body, leading to more injuries. According to a study conducted at the North Carolina School of the Arts, modern dancers had twice as many cervical and upper-back strains as ballet dancers. In contrast, ballet dancers reported close to 50 percent more strains to the lower back and hamstrings, as well as a higher number of shin splints than their modern-dance counterparts. Imagine all of the injuries you might face by mixing different techniques. Switching from pointe shoes to bare feet (without the protective calluses that modern dancers develop as they work shoeless), performing innovative choreography, and using alternate muscle groups can really catch you off guard.

Popular television programs such as *So You Think You Can Dance* demonstrate on a national stage the virtues and demands of being multifaceted as a dancer. The judges of this competitive reality show are looking for an employable, versatile dancer who can perform everything from hip-hop to ballroom dance. In 2007, the runner-up to the winner was a twenty-two-year-old male dancer who had performed in both ballet and contemporary companies before going on to do the show's fifty-city national tour after the final broadcast. Company dancers also switch genres by doing Broadway musicals like *Fosse, The Lion King,* and *Movin' Out.*

Meanwhile, preprofessional dance students are preparing to enter the work arena by enrolling in intensive training programs that include several techniques, and doing experimental workshops by the likes of Tony Award–winning choreographer Bill T. Jones. In the latter case, one eighteen-year-old dance student with years of ballet, modern, tap, African, and jazz under her belt was able to perform, but

OPENING THE DOOR TO PEAK PERFORMANCE

not name, this choreographer's eclectic movements. The steps simply weren't in her vocabulary.

These changes, while all well and good for dance as an art form, have personal costs for performers, who are taxing their bodies to the limit. In terms of survival, the old-fashioned approach to tough it out no longer applies to today's athletic dancer. The question is, how can dancers excel and still protect their bodies?

Shifting the Focus to Wellness at NYCB

To answer this question, I worked with experts from New York City Ballet's medical team to help reduce the rate of serious problems and disability. Similar to the rest of the profession, our company's dancers are taxing their bodies in ways never experienced by previous generations. NYCB rehearses and performs between thirty-eight and forty-three weeks a year. During this time, our dancers do everything—ballet, modern, musical theater, you name it. A dancer may perform George Balanchine's neoclassical ballets, Jerome Robbins's homage to Broadway, Peter Martins's contemporary movements, and modern works from the company's Diamond Project for experimental choreographers—all in one night! Our main objective as NYCB's medical team is to help the performers meet these demands by providing the latest interventions in dance medicine. We tackled this goal by taking a stepwise approach:

- Increasing on-site health services to provide immediate medical care and education

- Identifying challenges that create occupational stress using a confidential survey

- Creating a holistic wellness program to address mental, physical, and nutritional needs

- Measuring our progress by documenting workers' compensation claims

From all accounts NYCB's wellness program has been a resounding success for dancers' health and well-being. Workers' compensation claims for being completely "out" are down 26 percent, with 46 percent fewer weeks lost to disability. In addition, our research has identified ways to overcome common challenges in dance, providing the basis for our five keys to peak performance. Finally, NYCB's expenses for annual insurance premiums (which are a problem for most dance organizations) have decreased dramatically because of fewer workers' compensation claims.

This turnaround in the company has come about because we provided services that targeted our dancers' need to prevent injuries and achieve peak performance. Obviously, outside of NYCB each dancer's situation differs. However, we believe that it is possible to duplicate the major parts of our wellness program by enacting the following guidelines. Here is a brief preview of how you as a dancer can use this book.

Health Services

In this book you'll find a number of ways to stay healthy by catching problems early. In fact, seeking timely medical help for injuries is crucial to a dancer's survival (see box). Why? According to NYCB orthopedist Dr. William Hamilton, many musculoskeletal problems are resolved during the first month with proper diagnosis and treatment. While he considers this initial month "a magic healing period," it can

---

When to Seek Medical Help

WILLIAM G. HAMILTON, M.D.

- Pain limits certain dance movements for more than three to five days

- Joint(s) pop out, give way, or fail to provide support

- Pain continues during routine activities, such as walking or sleeping

- Pain gets worse over time

- Inability to bear body weight after a fall

---

disappear if you ignore the symptoms. Sadly, this scenario happened to Emily, a talented sixteen-year-old dance student with chronic groin pain who finally visited her orthopedist and learned that she had torn the cartilage around the rim of her hip (called the labrum)—two years ago! Rather than benefiting from conservative treatment—rest and physical therapy—this young dancer now required arthroscopic surgery. The bottom line: It pays to know when to seek medical services, especially if you are a stoic dancer.

While many physical symptoms are not a cause for alarm, it is always wise to notice pain. If any of Dr. Hamilton's criteria for seeking medical help apply, do not try to handle the problem on your own. You can locate a doctor or physical therapist who works with dancers by contacting the International Association for Dance Medicine & Science. The resources in Appendix A provide additional information about where to find health insurance, health-care referrals at a sliding scale, and emergency student loans.

Education

Becoming educated about your body is a central theme in this book. "People have a misconception that because you're a dancer, you know everything about your body," says NYCB physical therapist Marika Molnar. But, she explains, "You may not really know your body anatomically, kinesthetically, physiologically speaking. You know that you can lift one leg higher than the other, but you don't know why or what to do to make it work better." Many dancers have asymmetries or other minor problems like tight hamstrings without knowing how to deal with them.

NYCB principal dancer Yvonne Borree is a prime example, admitting, "I've had a rough battle with my foot throughout my whole career." For no apparent reason her foot will hurt while moving from flat foot to relevé. This can be due to many problems, including tendonitis. In Yvonne's case, says Molnar, it arose from cuboid subluxation, where the small cube-shaped bone on the outside of the midfoot shifts. This is a frequently misdiagnosed condition, and dancers may limp around in pain for months, or worse, get stuck in a cast because their medical provider is unfamiliar with the problem. Fortunately, Yvonne learned that whenever she experiences this strange sensation of pain and weakness, all she requires is a simple manipulation by a physical therapist to snap the bone back in place. For those of you with similar symptoms, ask your therapist to check out the Marshall and Hamilton article (listed in the bibliography, at the back of the book). Note: It is always a good idea to seek a second opinion and have your doctors confer if an injury isn't getting better. Appendix B provides a description of different medical professionals, diagnostic tests, anatomical terms, and common dance injuries.

Annual Screenings

The next step is to get screened before an intense dance program or season. After all, if top-notch athletes like the New York Knicks can benefit from yearly screenings, so can dancers. NYCB's wellness program focuses on general health, as well as orthopedic, fitness, and hypermobility issues to help identify and address potential problems. For example, in his fitness screenings NYCB's chiropractor, Dr. Lawrence DeMann, Jr., often finds subtle muscle imbalances in dancers that respond to an individualized exercise program at the gym.

You do not need to be a member of the company to have access to annual screenings. Just check out Chapter 3 to find out how they work. Then ask a dance medicine specialist to follow the screening protocols outlined in Part 3. NYCB's nutritional evaluation, which we describe in general terms in Chapter 2, will vary depending on the individual dietician. The key is to match your physical needs with the demands of dancing. Remember, the more you know, the better the odds of avoiding serious problems throughout your career.

Peak Performance

NYCB's wellness program includes annual workshops on the specific areas of concern that are the heart of this book: the five keys to peak performance. These universal keys apply to all types of dancers. Here's what we find works best.

1. **GOOD WORK HABITS.** Rather than forcing yourself to perform back-to-back technique classes or demanding choreography, it pays to prepare your body for exercise. This means knowing how to warm up, stretch, cool down, pace yourself, and deal with the normal aches and pains of dancing while taking your unique body into account.

2. **CROSS-TRAINING ACTIVITIES.** While these exercises can improve your level of fitness, they may undermine your performance if done incorrectly. It helps to know how to achieve your objectives, such as increasing stamina without adding unnecessary muscle bulk—a major concern for female dancers.

3. **EATING RIGHT TO STAY FIT.** Of paramount concern for dancers whose demanding schedules make it difficult to find or prepare the right foods, it's important to know how to eat in all kinds of circumstances to meet your health, fluid, and energy needs.

4. **EFFECTIVE WEIGHT CONTROL STRATEGIES.** As you might suspect, this area is a mine field—even the smartest dancers sometimes succumb to the latest fad diets. Understanding the basics of weight management helps prevent eating problems and brittle bones.

5. **STRESS MANAGEMENT TECHNIQUES.** Perhaps the greatest challenge for stoic dancers, you need to know how to deal with physical and mental stress to get into the "zone" to perform at your peak.

What This Book Will Do for You

Like most challenging careers, dancing requires you to seek a balance between work and downtime. NYCB's wellness program is a perfect remedy for all dancers who want to excel without compromising their health. The company is a microcosm of the demanding versatility that we have seen in the art form at large. With this book, serious dancers everywhere, not just those in NYCB, will be able to duplicate the main components of our program. Succeeding in today's dance scene involves life-changing approaches based on the latest advances in dance medicine. This book describes exactly how to not only avoid problems but build yourself into a more effective athlete *and* artist. I am here to teach you the principles of wellness that NYCB's dancers have learned. They can do it—and I will show how you can do it, too, with insights, physical screenings, resources, diaries, and even a "dancer's kitchen" for those of you who are cuisine-challenged.

Quiz: What's Your Wellness IQ?

We all know that dancers like to tough it out. However, to find the best way to use this book as a guide to a longer, healthier career, please consider the following questions:

1. When was your last screening for an orthopedic, fitness, and nutritional evaluation?

2. How do you prevent multiple injuries to the same body part?

3. Are there ways that you protect yourself from common precursors to stress fractures?

4. Do you have a cross-training program that suits your body throughout the year?

5. Are you aware of the proper care and shoe size for your foot type?

6. What is the healthiest approach to altering your weight?

7. Which foods help you recover from intense exercise and promote healing?

8. How do you tailor your current lifestyle to prevent overtraining and burnout?

9. What are your most effective tools for managing mental stress?

10. Can you be a person and be a dancer?

Read on to learn how you can meet your personal needs through our research, interventions, and the five keys to peak performance!

TWO

Common Challenges
for All Dancers

It's better to deal with your strengths and weaknesses before you get into a tough situation in dance.

—ADAM HENDRICKSON, NYCB soloist

While injuries are without a doubt a dancer's worst nightmare, the biggest revelation from New York City Ballet's research is that many challenges exist long before a dancer is incapacitated. Demanding schedules, emotional stress, worries about food, and difficult floors, costumes, and props top the list. A dancer's first instinct may be to ignore these problems; however, doing so can compromise both health and career. This chapter describes the common challenges that every dancer faces in order to excel in this profession.

Why is dancing so challenging? Because it requires all of a dancer's abilities, energy, and resources to handle the artistic and athletic demands, in addition to pleasing an audience. The dancer's deep connection to movement as a form of self-expression is all-encompassing. These demands apply not only to company dancers with extensive touring and performance schedules (such as NYCB) but to Broadway "gypsies" in musical theater, "commercial" dancers who do world tours with pop stars like Beyoncé, and aspiring professionals and students. The message from NYCB's wellness program is that it's okay for dancers—from ballet to tap—to have problems. These should not be seen as a sign of failure; they just need to be addressed.

LEFT (Adam Hendrickson in Eliot Feld's *The Unanswered Question*)

The Warning Signs in Dance

The biggest dilemma for many dancers is spotting the warning signs that lead to major problems. Before we focus on the findings from NYCB's survey, let's play detective by looking at three case studies of dancers who are experiencing occupational stress. Can you uncover each of their problems?

Amy is a seventeen-year-old ballet student enrolled in a six-week summer dance program. She's delighted to have passed the audition (scary!), even though it's intimidating to be surrounded by a roomful of talented dancers. A typical day begins at 9:00 A.M. and includes three to four technique classes. Amy tries to follow a nutritionally balanced 1,100-calorie meal plan because she wants to be thin enough to beat out the competition for a spot in the winter program. Yet she's gained five pounds over four weeks by pigging out on chocolate right before bedtime. What is she doing wrong?

Although you might jump to the conclusion that Amy's problem is nerves, let's take a closer look at her food intake. She currently eats a balanced meal plan (that is, healthy sources of carbohydrates, protein, and fats). However, there is a missing ingredient—calories! Without taking in a sufficient amount of food to balance her energy needs, cravings for sweets rule Amy's life, especially when her defenses are down late at night. The challenge: to increase her caloric intake by making sensible choices throughout the day without feeling guilty or compromising her weight goals.

Then there is Mike, who relies on the gym rather than dance class to stay in physical shape, since it can be months before he finds work in musical theater, where he sings, acts, and dances (known as the "triple threat"). After finally landing a Broadway show, which is like hitting the lottery, he is thrust into eight rigorous weeks of rehearsals. Tech periods follow (where they set the lights and scenery) and Mike is on standby for ten hours a day. He does one warmup and waits around to perform his routine with cold, stiff limbs. Previews of the show are the last chance to work out any kinks in front of a live audience before opening night. At this point, Mike's knees, which have had multiple injuries over the years, are killing him. What is he doing wrong?

Mike's rehearsal period is brutal. However, there is something more insidious going on that deserves attention. He is dancing himself into shape! This is asking for trouble. While it is a useful adjunct for getting fit, the gym does not provide the speed, coordination, and timing of executing technical steps in dance class. His knees are the first things to hurt (owing to prior injuries), plus he is not staying warm during tech days. The challenge: to be in top physical shape before he gets a job, while preparing his body to perform at a moment's notice with leg warmers and gentle warmup exercises.

The final scenario involves Sarah, who is in a modern dance company. Her days brim over with class, rehearsals, and performances that end at 11:00 P.M. She works hard, stays in shape, and does physical therapy exercises to prevent old injuries from recurring. Yet, in spite of being extremely conscientious, Sarah has begun to develop problems remembering new choreography. She is unaware of any personal concerns but often feels tired and takes frequent naps during the day. These help to revive her a bit for the next rehearsal. Sarah also makes sure to sleep at least seven hours per night but finds that during vacations her natural predilection is to sleep ten hours. What is she doing wrong?

Sarah's problems with remembering new choreography are recent, suggesting that she does not have a learning disability. She also stays in shape (unlike Mike). The tipoff is that she sleeps more than seven hours during vacations. This defines her true need for sleep (not counting the first few days of a vacation when she's working off her sleep debt). Dancing requires even more rest. As a result, Sarah is sleep-deprived, a problem that affects both her intellectual and her motor memory. The challenge: to get a sufficient amount of sleep during the season to enable her to perform up to her potential.

These cases highlight several of the many challenges that all dancers face. As you will see, some of the signs are subtle whereas others are more blatant. Regardless of the problem, it helps to be aware of the consequences and catch it early. Check out the following findings from NYCB's research to find out if any apply to you.

Overwork and Fatigue

Most serious dancers have schedules that overwork them to one degree or another. This is an occupational hazard, and one a fit, healthy dancer—a dancer who has absorbed the principles of wellness outlined in this book—can usually sustain. However, at the time of our survey the performers at NYCB were like many dancers whose work patterns inadvertently undermine their goals. These patterns included (1) adding cross-conditioning to an already busy workweek and (2) jumping into a strenuous training schedule after a break without being in physical shape. In both cases, these habits led to an imbalance between physical exercise and the body's ability to recover, creating extreme fatigue.

Why is it so bad for a dancer to drift into a fatigued state? Because it can lead to a host of problems (including burnout), according to dance medicine specialist Marijeanne Liederbach. For starters, chronic fatigue results in weaker muscles that are less able to protect your joints. It also takes a toll on your immune system. Besides prolonging the healing of injuries, excess fatigue increases the rate and severity of upper-respiratory infections, allergies, flulike illnesses, and one-day colds. Fatigue was a major cause of injuries in our survey. The good news is that it is possible to overcome the challenge of a busy dance schedule by practicing sensible work habits. NYCB dancers who paced themselves, like ballerina Yvonne Borree, were less likely to report fatigue or suffer health problems. "I would be injured if I went to the gym during the season," she says. Yvonne does her cross-training only on company breaks.

The Insidious Impact of Mental Stress

Few dancers realize that constant worries, whether about the quality of one's performance or about career, finances, or family, create another challenge to surmount. Yet the body's response to chronic stress is similar to fatigue. In addition to compromising your immune response (yes, expect more colds), stress hormones make it difficult to concentrate or relax. At NYCB the most stressful event was learning new choreography, followed by a full load of rehearsals and performances. Ellen Bar, who was in the corps at the time of our survey, recalls the strain she felt performing a solo variation in *Sleeping Beauty.* "It's a strenuous mental state because of the pressure to do well in a special role as well as whatever corps roles you have that night. You can't really focus on just one thing. You know, you're usually doing your [featured role] when you're already exhausted."

The dilemma for stressed-out dancers is that it is often difficult to stop worrying and get a good night's sleep, thus adding to their problems. Besides interfering with the ability to learn and remember new steps, lack of sleep slows reaction time. It's as if you had just polished off two martinis! It also affects your waistline. Professor Eve Van Cauter's research at the University of Chicago shows that sleep deprivation influences appetite hormones, making you want to overeat by as much as 1,000 extra calories a day. Fortunately, our survey found that dancers who managed to rest and engage in stress-busting activities throughout the year, such as yoga or psychotherapy, experienced a reduction in emotional stress, better health, and more consistent performances.

Poor Nutrition: You Are What You Eat

NYCB's initial survey revealed another finding that caught our attention: A number of female dancers had a significant delay in the onset of puberty compared to the general population, reaching menarche at fifteen years, against the population average of twelve and a half years. This was associated with a higher rate of stress fractures. Other dancers stopped menstruating for three or more months. Because nutrition can play a crucial role in menstrual problems, we developed a second questionnaire about food intake for all new dancers who entered the company. We learned that the dancers struggled with several issues when it came to eating, including poor time management, confusion about fad diets, and reliance on quick fixes like M&Ms for a sugar high that inevitably led to an energy crash.

Dancers need to eat for strength and energy, as well as to heal from injuries. This is why it is important to create a well-balanced meal plan to meet the athletic aspects of dance. While misconceptions about food and hydration are rampant among dancers, as well as in society at large, those who know about nutrition discover that food is an ally in their quest to excel. This was the case for principal dancer Ashley Bouder, who credits nutritional counseling with her ability to manage her weight without compromising her energy or health.

Costumes and Floors: The Occupational Hazards

The final challenge has to do with a dancer's work environment, beginning with a floor that is neither too hard (as in linoleum on concrete) nor too bouncy. While floors have come a long way, with special products from companies like the American Harlequin Corporation (www.harlequinfloors.com), little things can still get in the way.

According to former production stage manager Perry Silvey, NYCB uses a resilient (or sprung) floor based on an internal basketweave wooden construction to absorb the shock of landing from a jump. Yet, while he is happy with this setup in the studio, the stage floor is harder than he would like because it must be able to support heavy scenery. The portable dance floor that the company brings on tour also cannot completely compensate for a hard or poorly constructed floor at another location, often causing shin splints, tendonitis, or stress fractures. (See Appendix B for injury definitions.) The vinyl covering (formerly called marley) can cause problems too. When the dancers use too much rosin on the soles of their shoes, it remains in clumps on the stage, making the cleaner areas feel slippery. This can lead to falls.

Awkward props, toe shoes, and costumes place additional stress on the body. NYCB soloist Adam Hendrickson had an unrecognized weakness in his back, which created problems when he had to perform somersaults over a drum. He addressed this injury in physical therapy to protect himself from future problems. Toe shoes cause a different problem for female dancers, who have a higher rate of foot injuries. Partly, this risk is due to the hypermobility (or loose joints) associated with a good pointe position. Dancing on toe adds to the risk of injury.

Because you are balancing on a hard tip about the size of a silver dollar, it is easy to twist your foot if you slip. The solution is to be aware of this vulnerability, especially if you have had a previous ankle sprain, and strengthen the muscles around the joint to provide protection. *The Pointe Book,* listed in Appendix A, is an excellent resource for dancers who have questions about toe work. Heavy costumes also overload certain muscles; ankle-length brocade skirts can put a strain on the hips of dancers who are out of shape.

Awareness of this challenge is key. Dancers who back off from jumping on hard floors during rehearsals or address physical weaknesses with remedial exercises when faced with awkward props, toe shoes, and heavy costumes are less likely to falter even if they run through a blizzard of paper snowflakes. Now, if only they would use less rosin!

A Recipe for Injury

Put all these challenges together and you have an injury waiting to happen. While not all of them are under individual control, many are, and this book will help dancers take charge of those that are preventable. This is what happened to injured dancers Abi Stafford and Megan LeCrone, who learned the hard way how to gain control through NYCB's wellness program.

Abi and Megan:
From the Injury Trap to Recovery

Abi Stafford and Megan LeCrone both suffered foot injuries while rehearsing new choreography. For each of these women rehab, not surgery, was the treatment of choice, as the initial diagnostic tests showed relatively minor problems.

Abi's hypermobile ankles made dancing in toe shoes precarious, as she found out after landing badly from a jump in *The Nutcracker*. "I have loose ankles, so rolling over is something I do often," she recalls. "I'd just never done it this drastically." The MRI, which shows soft-tissue damage like slices of a loaf of bread, revealed a grade 2 ankle sprain with a completely torn and a partially torn ligament. Abi was out of commission for six weeks, with several more weeks of physical therapy on the horizon before she could resume dancing.

Up until her injury, Abi's career had seemed like a fairy tale. Promoted to soloist two years after joining the company, Abi had performed numerous ballerina roles, as well as winning the Martin E. Segal Award for her exemplary achievements as a young artist. She showed the same dedication during her rehab and tried to come back in the spring season, but her foot "didn't feel right." Dr. Hamilton and his partner, Dr. Phillip Bauman, ordered a second MRI with thinner slices. The results showed additional pathology that had been missed the first time, including a bone chip and a small defect in her ankle. It was a relief to finally have an answer to her pain and a plan of action. Her injury required arthroscopic surgery to drill and fill in the hole, just like a cavity in a tooth. Afterward, a cast and six weeks on crutches were necessary to let it heal.

Abi was forced to pace herself, particularly throughout her five months of rehabilitation, to regain motion and strength. Even when she felt as though she could push herself on pointe, her calf was not always ready. Abi had to be patient about getting back to a full class schedule. "My biggest regret is that I didn't get the other MRI sooner to know if my ankle was really okay. Maybe part of it was that I didn't want to know if there was another problem. I just wanted to get back to dancing. I was sort of in denial about it."

The second dancer to experience the same frustrating recovery was corps member Megan LeCrone—only this happened almost as soon as she entered the company. She had been accepted into NYCB's affiliated School of American Ballet three months before becoming a company apprentice, and she received her contract the following year. Megan then began to understudy a number of solo parts. She remembers thinking, "This is your chance to prove yourself. If someone goes out, you want to be prepared." She worked all the time and found the process nerve-wracking. One of the challenges associated with injuries in our survey was mental strain. However, since high achievers tend to be under some level of mental strain all the time, it can be difficult to determine when you need to ask for emotional support.

By failing to get educated about her body, Megan was unaware that her vulnerable areas included loose ankles and tight calves. While this combination may sound strange, only about 15 percent of the company's dancers are hypermobile in many joints, a condition known as benign joint hypermobility syndrome (BJHS). It is more common to have a mix of both loose and tight joints, as well as muscle imbalances that affect the joints. Like so many other dancers, Megan ignored pain and fatigue and was not wary of having a recurring injury, even though she had suffered a grade 2 ankle sprain in her right foot as an apprentice. This time, as a full-fledged member of the company, she felt pain in the same foot but chose to dismiss it. The injury came during an evening performance and left her unable to dance. She was initially diagnosed with acute tendonitis from a strained flexor hallucis longus (FHL) tendon, which she was told would take a few weeks to heal.

Meanwhile, the MRI, which can often diagnose soft-tissue problems (CT scans focus on bones), revealed nothing serious. Because it continued to hurt, Megan had numerous tests over the next ten months, but only a diagnostic injection to temporarily numb the pain revealed a serious problem: a tear in the FHL tendon. In some cases, anesthetic injections are more effective than MRIs in making a correct diagnosis in tendons, especially now that doctors use ultrasound (sonography) to identify the exact location of the injury. The end result: Megan was headed for surgery, physical therapy, and much-needed sessions to manage mental stress. She also visited a nutritionist, who encouraged her to increase her protein intake to speed up her physical recovery.

All was well when Megan returned to dance six months after her surgery—until she slipped during a rehearsal doing a minor step. Her "bad" foot had been completely rehabilitated, but her left ankle, which was also hypermobile, suffered a grade 2 sprain (a torn ligament with some instability). After four months of rehab she went back to dancing, while stabilizing both joints with daily exercises that helped her withstand another slip in a pile of snow during a *Nutcracker* rehearsal. This time it was a grade 1+ (a partial tear of one ligament), which took five weeks to heal.

Megan's biggest regret is her perfectionism. "I used to think, 'If

I just work harder than anyone else in the world, I can make it.' Not true! If I had found a way to manage each stressful situation instead of trying to prove myself every day, maybe I wouldn't have had such a big injury. It forced me to accept not being perfect."

Fortunately, she says, "I learned a lot of things in the time I was injured that made me a better dancer." Now she pays attention to her body and does daily remedial exercises. She also works on her perfectionism. "You have to let go of the stuff you can't control—the casting or if a new, good dancer joins the company—because it doesn't change you." Needless to say, she is a lot less stressed.

These stories are not atypical as they encompass the many challenges faced by dancers, including overwork, mental strain, nutritional concerns, slippery floors, toe shoes, and the hazards of ungainly costumes and tricky sets. They also highlight the importance of knowing your body's vulnerabilities.

Challenges are a fact of life in dance. Yet the more you know about your body's weaknesses, the better equipped you are to pick up the warning signs before problems become serious. NYCB's wellness program frees dancers to reach their potential as athletes and artists. Become proactive and you can overcome common challenges by taking a holistic approach to healthy dancing.

Highlights Revealed in Our NYCB Survey

- Ninety-six percent of the dancers reported an average history of four injuries.

- A heavy work schedule (more than five hours per day) was associated with new injuries due to fatigue.

- Women had more foot problems, whereas men had more knee and shoulder injuries.

- Poor physical conditioning during breaks predisposed dancers to new injuries.

- Mental strain from a variety of sources was a precursor to becoming injured.

- Dancers who stayed in shape and practiced stress management remained injury-free.

THREE

A Holistic Approach to Healthy Dancing

Dancing requires a combination of everything—the right foods, physical conditioning, and a positive attitude.

—KAITLYN GILLILAND, NYCB corps

O vercoming the challenges in dance is critical to your health, well-being, and success. Unfortunately, many dancers learn this lesson only after they experience a serious problem. New York City Ballet corps member Kaitlyn Gilliland is a poster girl for changing her entire approach to dancing after fragmenting the articular knee cartilage on the joint's surface at the age of seventeen. By using NYCB's annual screenings and available resources, Kaitlyn not only recovered from her injury but, in spite of the low odds, went on to land a leading role in Eliot Feld's *Étoile Polaire*. Though she was a fledgling apprentice, she got rave reviews and her photo in *The New York Times*. This chapter highlights ways to reduce the risks of a dancer's life outlined in Chapter 2 by taking a holistic approach to healthy dancing, rather than having to troubleshoot major problems after the fact.

One leading dancer told me that he would have made fewer mistakes taking care of his body if there had been a handbook called *Dancing for Dummies*. Well, here is your handbook—although dancers are no dummies! You are smart, goal-oriented high achievers who want to fulfill your dreams. The road to healthy dancing begins with establishing a lifestyle that supports your goals, based on the pillars of wellness. You will then be ready to use the clear,

LEFT (Kaitlyn Gilliland in Eliot Feld's *Étoile Polaire*)

easy-to-follow guidelines discussed in Part 2. Remember: Correcting problems is only one half of your arsenal of dance tools; the other half is living a healthy lifestyle.

The Pillars of Wellness

While many factors make up a healthy approach for dancers, the basic ingredients include education, coping skills, social support, and mind-body resources. These pillars of wellness, or foundations, will help you make wise choices in response to changing circumstances. For example, it's smart to adjust your lifestyle to meet different needs during performances, breaks, and auditions. The same goes for taking your anatomy and stage of life into account. A final area that benefits from sensible decision making involves fatigue, burnout, illness, and injury. To see how to create a healthy lifestyle, check out the basic elements.

EDUCATION. Serious dancers are perpetual students who believe in lifelong learning—at least when it comes to technique. However, it pays to educate yourself about your body's strengths and weaknesses by getting a physical screening. Ellen learned that the reason she could perform high kicks to the back was because she had loose joints. While this body type is an asset as a child (dance schools love flexible students), hypermobility makes you prone to injuries at the advanced level of training. The physical therapist who screened Ellen gave her special stability exercises to protect her joints. An annual screening can also pinpoint residual tightness or weakness from a prior injury, as well as help you improve your fitness level before starting a difficult season or dance program. The last pillar of wellness, mind-body resources, lists various specialists who can administer these tests. Additional educational sources, such as DVDs, are listed in Appendix A.

COPING SKILLS. It's equally important to cope with the challenges in dance by using a range of mental skills to manage both physical and emotional stress, rather than resorting to self-destructive behaviors such as overwork or worse! Allen was alarmed when his personal stress barometer went through the roof after he was promoted to soloist. He had always been a talented dancer, yet he worried about whether he was "good enough" to perform leading roles. Most gifted people, including dancers, are perfectionists who often set unrealistic goals that are impossible to achieve. Keeping your expectations in perspective is essential. In Allen's case, he counteracted his self-doubt by working with a cognitive-behavioral psychologist who taught him to set challenging but realistic goals, use positive self-talk to counteract his inner critic, and reframe his promotion in a more positive light (see it as an opportunity to grow as an artist). Further ways to reduce stress include balanced meals, aerobic exercise, and sufficient sleep (ten hours per night is ideal).

SOCIAL SUPPORT. Having positive people around you who support a healthy lifestyle is another pillar of wellness. Jackie never questioned her sensible eating habits until she entered a college dance program, where a group of students obsessed with being thin were living on coffee, cigarettes, and chocolate M&Ms. Realizing that she was starting to skip meals because she felt self-conscious around food, she switched to a different circle of friends, who knew that nutritious food revs up your metabolism and prevents binge eating. Social support also helps with other problematic behaviors, from smoking to substance abuse (see Chapter 4). Finally, having a group of friends can combat isolation and help prevent burnout, which is especially important on tour or if you live far away from your family. Dancers who find it difficult to reach out to others may benefit from joining community or religious centers or pursuing hobbies that bring them in contact with like-minded people.

MIND-BODY RESOURCES. A healthy lifestyle in dance depends on not only making the right choices but also having access to appropriate resources. Apart from working with a good dance teacher, these include:

- Rejuvenating activities, such as massage and acupuncture

- Medical, nutritional, and psychological services

- Cross-training sessions like yoga or Pilates

- Self-help information from books, Web sites, documentaries, etc.

Obviously, contact information is crucial. Miriam, who is a freelance dance teacher and performer, discovered that the International Association for Dance Medicine & Science's Web site offered a variety of resources, ranging from fact sheets on nutrition to books referencing research papers on every topic in the field and an extensive summary of IADMS's annual conferences. Dancers who want to locate a medical specialist in their geographic area can seek referrals from the executive director of IADMS, as well as the American Academy of Orthopedic Surgeons, the American Physical Therapy Association, and the American Dietetic Association. The American Psychological Association provides referrals for mental health specialists. (Contact Web sites are listed in Appendix A.)

As you can see, creating a healthy lifestyle takes both time and money. A decent survival job can do wonders; however, you need to be prepared. Many dancers have gotten certificates to be aerobic instructors at health clubs by taking home-study courses from the American Council on Exercise. Others work at Starbucks, which provides health insurance for part-time employees, or make do by catering on the weekend. The resources section in the back lists additional sources for health insurance and medical providers that offer dancers a break.

Developing a Healthy Lifestyle That Works for You

As you can see, many factors go into creating a holistic approach to healthy dancing. At its core are the pillars of wellness. These include education, coping skills, social support, and resources for your mind and body that will be used throughout this book. Furthermore, NYCB's proven screening protocol, outlined in the following section, can be used by a competent physical therapist or trainer to identify potential problems in all dancers. A general health, injury, and training questionnaire assesses basic parameters for dancers, combined with standard manual tests for orthopedic deficits, physical fitness, and hypermobility. Our nutritional evaluation is adapted for each dancer. Consequently, we offer general guidelines below, with considerable leeway for specific weight goals and preferences.

By helping dancers improve their overall conditioning while addressing any underlying mental or physical vulnerabilities, our wellness program emphasizes a healthy lifestyle. This includes counseling sessions and lectures given by the medical team. In my sessions I often focus on mental skills to help dancers cope with issues like performance anxiety, burnout, and stress management. In addition, the current company nutritionist, Joy Bauer, R.D., educates the dancers about ways "to keep their energy up and optimize their performance." Although dancers who are not naturally thin may also need to monitor their weight, Bauer emphasizes, "they can still have incredible energy and maintain muscle mass." Here is how this works.

The Orthopedic Screening

As you will learn in Chapter 5, recurring injuries, such as a sprained ankle, are common in the absence of sufficient rehab. Apart from examining the dancer's general health, training, and injury history, the orthopedic screening picks up structural and functional deficits (see Appendix C). For example, dancers with poor turnout in their hips (a structural problem) may eke out a few more degrees in ballet positions that require external rotation by "rolling in" their feet and ankles. This situation puts excessive pressure on the lower leg, knee, hip, and back, often creating tendonitis (a functional problem). If left uncorrected, this habit can lead to an acute injury, such as a torn knee cartilage, when landing badly from a jump. Similarly, dancers with unequal turnout, pointe, or relevé may get into trouble by trying to make their "bad" side look exactly like the good one. A common case is the dancer with a poor pointe in one foot. Frequently, the hidden problem is an extra bone in the back of the ankle (known as an "os trigonum"). Forcing it to improve by sitting on your foot or hooking it under a piano leg (please say no to those tricks!) can lead to chronic pain that may require surgery. The remedy for most structural problems is to work within your physical limitations, preferably under the guidance of a physical therapist.

Other functional problems, including tight hamstrings, also benefit from physical therapy. The hamstring spans two joints (the hip and the knee), so it is used in almost every movement of the lower body. This area is more likely to be injured when it is tight, as a result of growth spurts, structural asymmetries, or muscle strength imbalances. A stretching regimen can prevent a serious injury in these instances.

Another correctable problem is the labral tear in the hip (similar to a torn knee cartilage). Before the advent of MRI with a special hip coil that diagnoses soft-tissue damage of the labrum, dance medicine specialists mistook this injury for iliopsoas tendonitis, or inflammation of the hip. Now they know that the labrum can tear and may result in pain and premature wearing out of the hip joint, leading to degenerative arthritis (and a potential hip replacement in the distant future) if left untreated. Interestingly, these injuries often occur in dancers with excellent turnout, due to shallow hip sockets that have a large acetabular labrum (hip cartilage), which stabilizes the joint by extending the rim of the hip socket.

The last aspect of the orthopedic screening focuses on common foot problems that require major TLC. For example, bunions, which are especially prevalent in women, affect as many as 53 percent of top-level professional ballet dancers. While a number of factors have been implicated, such as heredity and tight shoes, a bunion is not caused by dancing on pointe. The most persuasive explanation is a genetic predisposition. This is referred to as a "simian" foot. We recommend that the bunion-prone dancer wear wide shoes and a spacer between the big toe and second toe to keep it better aligned. Bunion surgery is not an option for dancers until retirement, because removing bunions can limit the motion in the joint and ruin the demi-pointe relevé. Your practitioner will help you identify areas that can be corrected by physical therapy. Remember, prevention is best, so try to get screened *before* an injury occurs.

The Physical Fitness Screening

As dancing has become increasingly athletic, the need to be physically fit increased as well. The fitness screening focuses on three areas crucial to physical performance: cardiovascular fitness, physical strength, and flexibility (see Appendix D). We also check for muscle imbalances, where opposing muscles are either too weak or too strong, and hypermobility, both of which can lead to injuries. We give each dancer feedback, remedial exercises if necessary, and an individualized workout program. According to a number of dancers, the exercises have helped to prevent serious injuries. Many thought they were strong in places where they were really weak.

For example, if you are prone to knee injuries because of weak quadriceps, then you would need to do strength training at the gym. Upper-body weakness might call for twenty-five daily push-ups. For dancers with hypermobile ankles, like Abi Stafford and Megan LeCrone, stabilization exercises to strengthen the muscles around the joint, such as relevés and working the peroneal tendons, are helpful (see page 53). Flexibility, which is less of a problem in dancers than athletes, can vary for different muscle groups, as well as between the right and left sides. Again, appropriate exercises are needed to prevent tightness that can lead to muscle pulls. The last component of fitness is aerobic capability. This is rarely developed in dancers (because the movement is episodic), even though a cardiovascular workout can reduce the onset of fatigue—a major cause of dance injuries. Because most dance classes are filled with stops and starts, 41 percent of our dancers who did not go to the gym needed to have additional exercises, like workouts on an elliptical machine. To increase stamina, during breaks in the performance season they do thirty minutes of aerobic activity at least three times a week, working at their target rate. (See Chapter 6.)

For dancers like Abi, aerobic exercises were a great way to get in shape after her surgery. In addition to frequent physical therapy, she says, "I rode the bike even with my boot on!" This is not dangerous; post-op patients frequently ride bikes in a protective boot. Megan also went to the gym and remembers that her first dance class after she returned felt like she had never been out.

The Hypermobility Screening

One of the fundamental physical requirements for a dancer is to have an extensive range of motion to perform the choreography. However, there is a fine line between being flexible and being hypermobile. Although hypermobility is an asset in the selection process of young dancers, it can be a liability for professionals.

The current way to identify hypermobility in different areas of the body is based on the revised Brighton criteria for benign joint hypermobility syndrome. Dancers who are born with this syndrome often have unstable joints everywhere, as well as minor symptoms, such as loose, stretchy skin. Dance training can also cause specific hypermobility in the knee or ankle. In either case, a hypermobile joint is prone to injury and osteoarthritis, owing to less stability, coordination, and proprioception. The goal of this screening is to strengthen hypermobile joints with physical therapy. (See Appendix E.)

The Nutrition Evaluation

Because of the importance of a lean body in the dance world, food issues are a touchy subject for many dancers. Both men and women need guidance about keeping their energy up with nutritious meals. However, male and female dancers usually have different goals when it comes to weight. In general, women are more concerned with how to lose weight, while the men often need to build muscle. Injured dancers can also use nutritional counseling. For example, Megan discovered that her daily intake lacked sufficient protein to promote the healing process.

Our wellness program requires all apprentices to get a nutrition evaluation with the goal of offsetting potential problems. Each person receives a brief questionnaire, including personal and family medical history (such as diabetes or food allergies), a three-day food log, and a blank page to describe past experiences with food and weight. The dancers use this last page to explain their present situation and goals for the future. They then meet with a registered dietician who has extensive experience with dancers. This health-care professional takes into account various lifestyle issues, such as whether the dancer cooks, has dietary restrictions, smokes cigarettes, or has a current or past history of eating disorders.

The goal, which varies depending on the individual dancer, may be to lose weight or to maintain sufficient energy to perform. In all cases, the dancer and nutritionist should settle on mutually agreed-upon food guidelines. Yo-yo dieting, characterized by undereating followed by bingeing, is addressed by adjusting caloric intake throughout the day and trying to remove problematic trigger foods from the dancer's diet. Some dancers have trigger eating times, such as free days, which must also be dealt with. Liquid intake is important as well, because dancers who lose electrolytes and water from sweating need to stay well hydrated. While many foods, like cucumbers, have a high water content, drinking fluids, including water, is essential. Coffee in excess can be dehydrating, so try to drink water rather than six cups of Starbucks. NYCB soloist Ellen Bar admits, "It's something I fight with because I hate drinking water. I make myself do it." Hint: A squeeze of lemon juice adds flavor. Ideally, female dancers need to drink at least nine eight-ounce cups of fluids per day for moderate exercise, whereas male dancers require a minimum of thirteen eight-ounce cups. Certain liquids are better to drink before, during, and after dance, and one must know how to identify the rare but dangerous signs of overhydration.

To see how a screening profile works, take a look at the following results from one of the company's apprentices, whom we shall call John.

Sample of Screening Profile

John is an eighteen-year-old NYCB apprentice. His first appointment was with Dr. William Hamilton, the company's orthopedic consultant, for a general health and orthopedic screening. This twenty-minute evaluation, which included a questionnaire and physical exam, revealed a number of anatomical findings. John was knock-kneed and he had a poor relevé and insufficient turnout. In an effort to improve his fifth position, he forced his feet outward, causing him to roll in—a common problem in ballet. Fortunately he had not yet developed tendonitis or any other injuries from these habits, in spite of occasional pain.

Dr. Hamilton felt that John would benefit from a Pilates exercise program. This would strengthen the turnout muscles in his hips, while decreasing the tendency to roll over in his feet. He also referred John to the company's physical therapists to improve his technique and placement. (Note: Talent, *not* a perfect body, got John into NYCB.)

Of course, physical fitness is another story. While John could do twenty-five push-ups in the blink of an eye, he was surprised to learn that his deltoids and abdominals were weak. NYCB chiropractor Dr. Lawrence DeMann recommended that he correct these deficits with light weights at the gym to avoid unwanted bulk, along with Pilates exercises. John's fitness evaluation also showed physical therapist Marika Molnar that he needed to be in better cardio shape, given that his heart rate did not return to normal three minutes after jumping rope at high speed. The remedy was to use the elliptical machine three times a week for thirty minutes.

The good news: No problems were found for hypermobility or nutrition. A follow-up during the next season showed that John had followed the recommendations from his screening protocol and remained injury-free.

To conclude: By being willing to make a life change—to shift your approach to how you view your body and treat it—you can free yourself to become an artist. The pillars of wellness will provide a solid foundation for developing a holistic approach to healthy dancing. However, change is not an on-off switch. It is a process that requires overcoming roadblocks as you alter ingrained habits. This book will take you through this process as we navigate the road ahead.

FOUR

Keeping Your Eye on the End Goal

I've learned to keep my eye on the end goal. Even when I mess up, I try to let it go, and move ahead.

—ELIZABETH WALKER, NYCB corps

Did you know that only 40 percent of people who make a New Year's resolution keep it? Whether it's quitting a cigarette habit or eating more nutritious food, changing behavior is not an on-off switch. It is a multistage process where you may think about change, experiment with it, and go back and forth before you're ready to take action. Slipping back into an old habit that is ingrained, pleasurable, or comforting is also normal. Consequently, switching gears is difficult for even the most highly driven, motivated dancer because it takes more than your own willpower to make change happen—it takes strategies. This chapter gives you the tools to understand and embrace the process of change, and survive the bumpy ride.

Correcting a problematic behavior or adopting a healthier one requires that you give yourself a break by having realistic expectations. (Hint: Perfection isn't one of them.) This can be challenging for dancers who are used to being evaluated by how well they perform. Common stumbling blocks in dance include:

- Labeling yourself as "weak" if you have a problem, which may keep you from seeking help until you hit a major roadblock

LEFT (Elizabeth Walker and Albert Evans in Peter Martins's *Barber Violin Concerto*)

- Clinging to unhealthy habits to manage your weight, strive for perfection, or reduce occupational stress

- Feeling superstitious about updating your training routine, such as adding aerobic workouts, because the old way (e.g., just dance class) worked in the past

- Being afraid to adopt a new behavior and fail, especially if you are a perfectionist who has tried and failed before

- Worrying that you'll be given fewer opportunities by those in power if you seem to have problems

These obstacles are tied to losing face as a performer and a person. Former NYCB principal dancer James Fayette, who is now a union dance executive at the American Guild of Musical Artists, says, "I've been a victim of it myself. You want to focus on your strengths in dance [not what's wrong] to avoid feeling tentative as a performer." Still, he recognizes the benefits of stepping out of your comfort zone and taking advantage of the company's wellness initiative. The question is, where do you begin?

Psychologists James Prochaska, John Norcross, and Carlo DiClemente have identified specific stages in everyone—not just dancers—associated with altering a wide variety of behaviors. To move forward, you need to use strategies that match where you are right now for your most pressing problem. Take the following self-quiz to locate your current stage, and note the tactics that will help you move to the next stage and eventually achieve your goal.

Self-Quiz: What's Your Stage and Strategy for Change?

STAGE 1: You "don't think" about changing your behavior.
STRATEGIES: Learn more about it; benefit from social supports, like smoke-free zones or low-fat menus.

STAGE 2: You "think" about making a change but do not have a specific plan.
STRATEGIES: Notice negative outcomes; see how your behavior clashes with your view of yourself.

STAGE 3: You "prepare to change" within thirty days, using a realistic plan and time line.
STRATEGIES: Add additional assistance (e.g., hotlines or therapy); use educational self-help tools.

STAGE 4: You've "taken action" in the last six months, but may have had a few slips.
STRATEGIES: Commit to change; reward good behavior; expand support network; respond differently to triggers; restructure environment (e.g., replace candy with fruit).

STAGE 5: You've consistently replaced an old habit with a new one for over six months.
STRATEGIES: Same as stage 4. Bravo!

Putting the Show on the Road

Now that you have a general idea of where you are on the change continuum, it is important to use the strategies that will foster movement to the next stage. Be aware that few people are ready to take immediate action. Instead, it is more common to move back and forth several times between stages 1 and 3, where change isn't on your mind, you start to consider it, and eventually prepare a plan and time line to act within the next month. Focusing on two or three related behaviors, such as cardio, resistance training, and nutrition for healthy weight loss, will increase your chances of success. Trying to change more than three behaviors at once is counterproductive. Discover how the stages of change can work for you by following Carrie as she deals with her food cravings in a college dance program.

Stage 1: Precontemplation

Carrie is an emotional eater who uses candy and ice cream to cope with stress. After years of trying and failing to make better food choices, she feels hopeless about altering her behavior. Change is not on Carrie's mind, even though she's gained ten pounds. At this stage, the last thing Carrie wants to hear is practical advice about weight loss. Her mother's well-intentioned efforts to try to force her to go on a diet also do more harm than good. Carrie feels coerced into changing her behavior and eats more junk food. What does help her think about change? A lecture on eating problems at her college raises her conscious awareness and shows Carrie how other dancers thrive after addressing this issue. A newsletter on the topic from the dance department also helps her to learn more about the problem. Another tool that increases her consciousness involves the following two exercises in her health education course. The first requires that she create a list of the reasons why making healthier food choices might be helpful. Carrie wrote:

1. "I'll have more energy for dancing."

2. "Adding fruit and vegetables to my diet will help me get back to a healthy weight."

3. "I won't feel sick from eating three candy bars right before dance class."

In the second exercise, Carrie lists the reasons why she is not giving up junk food:

1. "I lack the willpower to change."

2. "Chocolate helps me cope with pressure."

3. "I want to have fun at the end of the day by eating ice cream."

Carrie decides to talk to a friend who has dealt successfully with her own food issues (another way to learn more about this behavior). The fact that the college cafeteria provides tasty alternatives to junk food (social support) makes it easier to eat a healthy lunch once in a while, as she begins to think about changing her behavior. (Note: The only time it is appropriate to force a dancer to take action at stage 1 is when his or her health requires medical intervention, as in the case of someone with anorexia nervosa or serious substance abuse.)

Stage 2: Contemplation

Just thinking about giving up junk food represents a giant leap forward for Carrie. Yet mixed feelings also rear their ugly head now that she is beginning to weigh the pros and cons of change. While ambivalent feelings pop up throughout the different stages, they are at full strength during stage 2. It is easy to get stuck here indefinitely. After all, Carrie's friends are giving her tons of positive reinforcement for her "good intentions," while she is feeling self-righteous because someday she will eat healthy food. The strategies that helped her to acknowledge her problem continue to be useful (i.e., intellectual awareness; social support). However, Carrie needs a strategy to arouse her emotions. A health crisis serves as a wake-up call. After eating candy all day, which results in an energy high that drops precipitously, Carrie tears her knee cartilage in a dress rehearsal for the school's choreographic workshop and has to sit out the performance. Arthroscopic surgery and six weeks of rehab hammer in the point. (Note: A personal crisis isn't necessary to increase your emotional awareness, as long as some event arouses strong feelings about the need to change.)

As Carrie buys into the notion, intellectually and emotionally, that her eating has to change, she needs to use a different strategy to correct the mismatch between her thoughts and actions. She sees herself as a serious dancer who wants to be a professional in musical theater. However, her eating behavior conflicts with her self-concept and threatens her aspirations.

Carrie speaks to the school nurse, who tells her that she can control her cravings, but also alerts her that she needs to be well prepared because change isn't easy. She asks her if there are any roadblocks standing in her way. Carrie thinks for a while and writes down three in her notebook, which she shares. These include:

1. "I don't know where to start."

2. "How do I deal with stress?"

3. "I know I can't do it alone."

The nurse is compassionate and understanding. She tells her that help is available at the campus counseling center, which is free for college students. (Professional dancers can also locate psychological services on a sliding scale by contacting the Dancers' Resource program.) For the first time, Carrie is truly hopeful that she can change her eating problem. The nurse's message of a brighter future, along with the reality that common discomforts accompany letting go of any problematic behavior, keep her from being blindsided by her fears. She makes an appointment with the therapist. Carrie is entering stage 3.

Stage 3: Preparation

At this stage, all kinds of options appear that Carrie either didn't see or failed to recognize until she finally decided to change. The extent to which she remains determined, motivated, and hopeful will have a major impact on later decisions, such as setting a time line and developing a plan. She uses therapy to realistically visualize the future without using food as an emotional crutch as in the past. Carrie rehearses success by learning how to use a variety of therapeutic tools, like relaxation exercises, to manage stress. (See Chapter 9 for more details.) She develops the coping skills of a controlled eater who can deal with stressful dance auditions and performances. Mentally rehearsing successful outcomes helps her to see the light at the end of the tunnel even in the face of periodic relapses.

Carrie's therapist also recommends further education and support in the preparation stage through online tools such as Overeaters Anonymous (www.overeatersanonymous.org), and self-help publications that focus on her health and eating problem. For example, she is able to get more information and help by logging on to OA and recognizing that others have the same problem that she does. In reading *Life Without Ed* (Ed = eating disorder), Carrie learns to treat her penchant for junk food as an abusive relationship from which she can eventually separate. All these strategies contribute to Carrie's written plan. This includes starting the day with a relaxation exercise, planning her daily menu, logging onto OA daily for online meetings, and locking Ed in the closet (so to speak) when she has a yearning to deal with her emotions with a candy bar or ice cream.

By using one-on-one counseling, education, and other self-help materials, Carrie not only moves into the action stage but increases her chance of lifelong change. She has created a realistic plan and set a date to change her behavior in two weeks, after a birthday party where she might be tempted to have too much cake. Carrie chooses July Fourth because of its special meaning—Independence Day! Be aware that each plan is specific to the individual. While psychotherapy helped Carrie successfully move to stage 4, most people change without the benefit of a formal support program. The exceptions are serious health problems, such as eating disorders and substance abuse.

Stage 4: Action

The good news is that Carrie has finally arrived; the reality is that her new behavior can last anywhere from one day to six months. Two characteristics define the action stage for Carrie: conflict and turmoil. Her intellectual side is struggling for change using facts, logic, and reason, but her emotions are fighting just as hard to soothe herself with sweets. It takes considerable energy and conscious thought to change her old behavior, often leaving her completely exhausted. Her burning desire to succeed keeps her going, but she always has to be on guard. Carrie adds the following strategies to help her out.

First, she takes responsibility for changing her eating patterns by making a public commitment to her friends and family, which is more powerful than making a private commitment to herself. Second, Carrie rewards herself every time she makes a decision to avoid candy in the face of stress by having her nails manicured or getting a back massage. Third, she constantly restructures her environment by filling her pantry with healthy treats, such as low-fat string cheese, yogurt, grapes, figs, and a single serving of her favorite snack that she replenishes daily. To avoid feelings of deprivation, no food is off-limits. The key is moderation. Fourth, Carrie keeps a food diary, where she records her feelings. This tool helps her note when she's vulnerable to emotional eating. (See Chapter 7 for a more detailed description.)

It is normal to relapse in the action stage. Carrie succumbs after auditioning for the lead role in a school production and feeling worthless after she isn't chosen. Fortunately, her therapist teaches her how relapses provide an opportunity to learn ways to avoid triggering the same behavior in the future. Carrie discovers that she is extremely sensitive to rejection. In fact, anyone who goes in front of an audience is taking a special risk. Dancers need corrections, but they also require affirmation. She must address this issue if she wants a career in musical theater. Her therapist teaches her to "reframe" situations like an audition as learning experiences (a cognitive technique). No dancer can control the outcome. However, Carrie can control her performance by warming up, remembering the choreography, and smiling at the judges. That way she can't lose. Carrie is graduating to the last stage.

Stage 5: Maintenance

It's been over six months since sweets dominated Carrie's life. Still, even though she is replacing her old habit with healthy eating, she worries about whether she can maintain this for the long haul. Carrie's therapist reassures her that it's both realistic and safer to be aware of possible pitfalls rather than being complacent. Her responses become automatic after a year of positive (or neutral) reactions to old triggers. While there are several sporadic incidents where she thinks of "sinful behavior," she is in control 99 percent of the time by continuing to use all of her strategies. Carrie celebrates her accomplishment, shares her story with other struggling dancers, and creates a list of the benefits she's had from healthy eating. She writes:

1. "I feel more confident as a dancer and a person."

2. "My energy level is consistent, with no more sugar highs or lows."

3. "I'm finally happy with my weight."

4. "I love dancing even when it's challenging."

Now that Carrie is maintaining healthy eating, she begins to look at other changes that might improve her career. She decides to focus on taking more risks by pushing her technique, with the goal of performing at her peak.

What About Abi and Megan?

The two injured NYCB dancers whom we are following throughout this book had succumbed to serious injuries at the onset of promising careers. They came to psychotherapy for stress management through the company's wellness program because they felt overwhelmed. Abi recalls, "I wasn't prepared for this freak accident. Suddenly, I was out [unable to dance] and on crutches. I was sleeping all the time. And the more I slept, the more tired I got." In contrast, Megan found herself struggling with mounting internal pressures to dance, even though her injury had yet to heal. Their dramatic injuries catapulted them to stage 3, where they made a plan to change how they coped with occupational stress, using cognitive-behavioral techniques like reframing their injury as an opportunity to cross-train and become a better dancer. They also focused on practicing good work habits that would protect them in the future, such as pacing themselves. Finally, Megan learned how to work with her perfectionism by setting more realistic goals. As you'll see, taking a healthy approach to dancing improved their performance when they were back on their feet and being featured in principal roles.

Understanding how change works can help you address self-defeating behaviors and harness your potential in dance and in life. You can refer back to the different stages and strategies, as needed. Whenever you envision a change of behavior, the hardest battle is within. However, even when you backslide, you can use this experience to learn different ways to cope in the future. Remember: You double your chance of success when you move to the next stage!

PART TWO

The Five Keys to Peak Performance Through Mind, Body, and Nutrition

FIVE

Good Work Habits

You're ambitious and want management to notice you. But there are ways to work that won't kill you.

—JOAQUIN DE LUZ, NYCB principal

How you work makes a huge difference in your success as a dancer—partly in avoiding injury, but also in achieving career longevity and that loftiest of goals, peak performance. Yet there is no uniform approach to working productively. Every dancer's body is different, with its own strengths and weaknesses. Consequently, it is crucial to develop work habits that suit your individual needs. This chapter shows you how to prepare your body for exercise by taking your physical characteristics into account.

In general, good work habits span a range of activities from warming up, stretching, and cooling down to sleeping, pacing, and dealing with the normal aches and pains from exercise. Unfortunately, dancers usually practice these habits after they become injured. NYCB principal dancer Joaquin De Luz knows this fact firsthand after undergoing knee surgery while performing in another company. "We've all been there—working too hard and never relaxing. My injury put things in perspective because I had to ask myself, 'What if I can't dance anymore?' [Now] I do all kinds of good things for my body like special warmups and little breaks during the day," he says. While good work habits cannot change your basic anatomy, such as the bony configuration of a hip joint, they can make you a far more effective dancer by correcting muscle imbalances and helping you gain the greatest functional strength, stamina, and range of motion for your body.

LEFT (Joaquin De Luz with, from left to right, Damian Woetzel, Amanda Edge, Seth Orza, and Jenifer Ringer in Jerome Robbins's *Fancy Free*)

Know Your Instrument

The first step in developing good work habits is to know your physical instrument (with all its quirks), including natural asymmetries and differences in strength, endurance, flexibility, the shape of the foot, and turnout. You also need to make adjustments during periods of vulnerability, such as an injury or adolescent growth spurt. It is a common misconception that young dancers can do anything, yet this group is more likely to develop a serious injury—an ankle fracture rather than just a sprain. When dancers shoot up a few inches, the growth plates widen at the end of the bones, making these areas two to five times weaker than the surrounding joints, ligaments, and tendons. Muscle strains (or pulls) are also more common as increases in size precede gains in strength. Another problem that can develop in teenage girls is curvature of the spine (scoliosis), especially if their menarche is delayed, as it is for most female dancers. These curves need to be followed carefully in case they progress and require treatment.

Teenage dancers may also go through an awkward period where they temporarily lose their technique. This happened to Matt, a sixteen-year-old ballet student who grew three inches in less than a year. During this time, he lost flexibility, balance, and coordination. The height of his arabesque was lower and he had more problems doing multiple pirouettes. Like most serious dancers, Matt would have worked harder to compensate if not for input from his instructor, who understood these problems after reading the resource paper "The Challenge of the Adolescent Dancer" from the International Association for Dance Medicine & Science. Dancers who are going through a rapid period of growth often need to cut back on jumps, partnering, and extra classes (no more than one to two easy classes per day). Likewise, they must accept these physical limitations not only to protect their self-esteem but to keep from forcing their leg extensions and turnout. Matt made appropriate adjustments by adding nonimpact workouts, such as swimming, gentle stretching, and Pilates with light weights to stabilize his trunk and ensure that his muscle groups were equally balanced. (Note:

Strength training is not recommended for young dancers before age twelve.)

Structural and Functional Asymmetries

While growth spurts are obviously no fun, adult performers have to contend with various asymmetries in size, strength, and flexibility after the skeleton matures (generally between the ages of eighteen and twenty-one for dancers). Lauren is a twenty-three-year-old performer in musical theater who has differences between the right and left sides of her body. Her dominant leg is 5 to 10 percent stronger, making it difficult for her to perform certain dance combinations. Anti-gravity muscles like the quadriceps in the front of the thigh are also stronger than the hamstrings in the back. Muscle imbalances can be corrected when diagnosed and treated under the guidance of a physical therapist, athletic trainer, or instructor in Pilates or another type of cross-training. (See Chapter 6.) In contrast, structural differences do not respond to exercise, although problems like differences in leg length of over half an inch that are symptomatic may benefit from a shoe insert, or orthotic. However, if it isn't bothering you, there's no need to fix it!

Other muscular imbalances may develop from dance technique. For example, pointe work tends to create stronger calf muscles than the opposing muscles in the front of the leg that bend the ankle and foot upward. Muscles that hold the leg out to the side (developpé à la séconde) can also be more developed than the opposing muscles that move the leg toward the midline. Finally, upper-body strength—crucial for partnering—is often neglected in ballet (unlike modern dance), because the technique emphasizes the lower limbs and feet. While correct posture is essential for partnering (that is, no swayback), most male ballet dancers require exercises to strengthen the upper body and core muscles that involve the abs, pelvis, and back. According to NYCB chiropractor Dr. Lawrence DeMann, "The taller the men are, the stronger they need to be because they're going to be lifting bigger women."

Good work habits must take your structural and functional imbalances into account. Yet you're still working in the dark until you know how to address genetic differences that affect muscular strength and endurance, flexibility, foot type and arch, and turnout—the necessary components of dance.

Muscular Strength and Endurance

Do you have strong bulky muscles that create an explosive jump but tire easily doing aerobic exercise? Or are you one of those long lean dancers who could easily run a marathon yet can barely get off the ground? The reason for these muscle differences lies in your genes. Each one of us is born with a mix of slow- and fast-twitch muscle fibers that make up every muscle group. While the typical ratio is one-to-one, special athletic abilities indicate that you may have more of one fiber type than another.

For instance, dancers who are able to leap and bound at a moment's notice are more likely to have a greater preponderance of fast-twitch fibers, which contract five to ten times more quickly than their slow-twitch counterparts. These fibers are also 30 to 40 percent bigger, creating a more muscular build. As a result, dancers with this genetic makeup can jump higher than their less muscular colleagues, but they become bulkier doing the same high-impact workouts. Meanwhile, performers with a preponderance of slow-twitch fibers will have greater aerobic endurance, which comes in handy in today's high-octane choreography. They may also have a more aesthetically pleasing body build for certain dance techniques like ballet. The problem is, their jumps are less powerful. What to do?

There is no way to change the actual distribution of your muscle fibers. However, you can make modifications in your performance and body type by how you choose to cross-train. Let's start with the dancer who is a high jumper with more of two types of fast-twitch fibers (A and B). By doing low-impact aerobic workouts on the elliptical machine, this dancer can transform fast-twitch type B fibers into type A. This accomplishes two goals: (1) creating larger type A fibers that enhance cardiovascular changes so skeletal muscles receive better supplies of oxygen and carbohydrates (for energy) and (2) minimizing muscle mass, helping this dancer to slim down.

The mistake that many muscular dancers make is to avoid aerobic exercise, while doing sprinting-type exercises like swimming for several minutes at a time. Yet this approach releases an exercise-induced growth hormone that increases the size of the muscles. In contrast, dancers who want to become more muscular should use sprinting exercises to increase their natural body-building steroids, in combination with lifting heavy weights to enlarge the diameter of fast-twitch type B fibers. (See page 83 for details on weight training.)

You will also need to strengthen loose joints that result from hypermobility or injury. For example, ankle sprain is one of the most common problems in dance. Once the ligaments that stabilize the ankle joint are torn (grade 2 and 3 sprains), they will not return to their normal length, thereby predisposing you to another sprain. The only way to protect the joint is to strengthen the surrounding muscles. Five to ten slow single-foot relevés throughout the day will strengthen the calf muscles. However, it is equally important to strengthen the peroneus longus and brevis muscles in the lower leg that stabilize the ankle on demi-pointe and on toe. Dancers Megan LeCrone and Abi Stafford, who had both suffered ankle sprains, initially did this under the instruction of a physical therapist. They learned to use the Theraband for resistance, while assuming the pointe position and winging the foot out to the side for three long seconds, counting "one thousand, two thousand, three thousand" in sets of ten, one to three times per day. Core strengthening and Pilates exercises are additional ways to protect the joints of hypermobile dancers.

Flexibility

The ability to move a joint through its full range of motion (ROM) allows you greater freedom to execute movements without incurring strained muscles or tendons. Yet hard work is not enough: 85 percent of flexibility comes from the architecture of your joints (which cannot be changed), whereas only 10 percent depends on the elasticity of your muscles. A mere 5 percent comes from such factors as age, gender, and the temperature in your environment.

As a result, range of motion varies dramatically from person to person but also within different body parts. These differences span a continuum from tight to flexible to loose-jointed and are predetermined at birth. Maria is a hypermobile jazz dancer who has ankles that sprain and leg extensions up to her ears. Her best friend's leg can barely hit ninety degrees, but she's never had an ankle sprain in her whole career. The moral of the story: While you may not be hypermobile in every joint, any extremes in range of motion come at a cost. Maria's hypermobility makes her prone to sprains and dislocations.

Tip

The Stork position, where you stand on a straight flat foot for sixty seconds without wobbling or putting your other foot down, is a way to assess strength and balance that is unlikely in hypermobile dancers.

How else can you tell if you are at risk for an injury from extreme joint mobility? Dr. William Hamilton says to watch out for ankles that constantly roll over, or kneecaps and shoulders that pop in and out, known as subluxation. Jane discovered that she had hypermobile knees after her patella (kneecap) subluxed during a rehearsal for a music video. Simple leg lifts do not take care of this problem. According to Marika Molnar, "You need to contract all the muscles around the knee to make the joint stable." A physical therapy program typically includes exercises like the imaginary chair, where you lean against the wall, squat, and strengthen all four muscles surrounding the knee until you tire.

Not surprisingly, tightness creates a different set of problems because it restricts your ability to move, leading to repeated muscle strains (or pulls). Apart from genetic differences, overwork can be your undoing. Tired muscles are much more prone to tightness. Dr. Yiannis Koutedakis, an exercise physiologist, and his colleagues found that total flexibility in professional ballet dancers increased by 15 percent after a six-week break. While getting looser by not dancing may seem counterintuitive, they speculated that accumulated fatigue or burnout causes muscles to get tighter during a performance season. Be aware that excessive stretching before class, performances, or athletic events can weaken your muscles. Taking advantage of warm weather or, worse, "hot" yoga in a saunalike studio to get a few more inches of length can tax fatigued muscles and leave you sore, tight, and prone to injury.

Foot Type and Arch

For dancers who work on pointe it is important to be able to feel the floor, so be wary of hard shoes and excess padding. According to podiatrist Dr. Thomas Novella, who sees over two hundred dancers a year, it is the fit, not the brand, of toe shoe that helps to prevent injuries. As a result, it is best to get your shoes sized in the morning before your feet swell. (The exception is gym sneakers, which need a half-inch space at the toe and should be fitted in the evening.) It takes at least three years of ballet training to develop sufficient strength, balance, coordination, and bone density to perform steps on toe. To avoid excess strain on the leg, you also need to be able to rise up in the vertical position and create a straight line between your pointed foot and leg. For more information, download the resource paper entitled "When Can I Start Pointe Work?" at www .iadms.org.

Broadway dancers, who may wear two- to six-inch heels, also benefit from the right shoe. Lest you think that you have found the perfect match, know that all types of dance shoes need to be resized during a rapid growth spurt, as well as every three years after the skeleton matures, because your feet tend to spread with age. Daily hygiene and proper nail clipping are essential for maintaining a healthy dancer's foot (see "Foot Care" on page 57).

Next, find out your own personal needs by assessing your foot type:

1. THE GISELLE (OR PEASANT) FOOT. The first three toes, which are close to being equal in length, require padding between them to prevent soft corns, as well as a wide toe box or shoe.

2. THE GRECIAN (OR MORTON'S) FOOT. The long second toe bruises easily on pointe without a foam toe cap plus padding that distributes the weight evenly across all the toes.

3. THE EGYPTIAN FOOT. The long big toe needs proper nail clipping to avoid ingrown toenails, a foam cap and spacer to keep it straight, and padding to spread the weight.

4. THE SIMIAN FOOT. A genetic bunion develops, requiring a donut-shaped foam pad, a spacer between the first two toes, and a wide toe box or shoe.

5. THE MODEL'S FOOT. The fifth toe is much shorter than the first in this thin, tapered foot; considerable padding is needed to compensate for the disparate lengths.

A final structural category involves your arch, the hollow part under the foot. Like most people, dancers tend to fall into three categories: the normal arch; the high arch, or cavus foot; and the low arch, or flat foot. As a general rule, "The higher the arch, the better the pointe," says Dr. Novella. Yet a high arch tends to have a shallow plié. The only way to create a deeper plié is by slightly lifting the heel after landing from a jump. Toe dancers also need to support the entire length of the foot with a full shank (the portion between the shoe's inner and outer sole). A three-quarter shank without the heel portion provides space for a bigger pointe for a normal arch but reduces the plié of a cavus foot even more. Finally, be aware that the cavus foot absorbs shock poorly because it is rigid, making it more likely to develop stress fractures. Your best protection is to have strong muscles, a solid technique, and a sprung floor.

The flat foot, on the other hand, has a very deep plié but a less dramatic relevé or arch; this may interfere with standing on toe in the vertical position. This foot is also more likely to develop tendonitis because it is hypermobile and tends to roll in. Physical therapy exercises can help control hypermobility and slightly improve your arch and vertical motion. However, please avoid jamming your foot into so-called toe stretchers. These bend the front part of the foot down and can injure loose ligaments. A safer approach is to attach specially designed pads on top of your feet to create the illusion of a higher arch (information on where to purchase these is listed in Appendix A). The best toe box for a flat foot is square.

Foot Care

DAILY HYGIENE

- Keep feet clean; remove dirt under toenails with a little wooden orange stick.

- Use pumice stone in bath or shower to prevent splits in calluses.

- Apply oil to lubricate calluses at night even if you dance in shoes.

- Use tincture of benzoin to toughen the skin.

- Protect bare feet from scrapes and cuts by taping them with Elastikon.

- Prevent blisters in shoes with moleskin.

- Reduce inflammation by soaking feet in hot water with Epsom salts.

INFECTIONS AND INCLUSION CYSTS (SCAR TISSUE AROUND GLASS, ETC.)

- Open large blisters with sterile needle on the edge, not at the center, leaving skin to act as a dressing.

- Remove superficial splinters or glass with sterile tweezers and a needle.

- Seek immediate medical help to remove embedded foreign objects.

- Clean open cuts with mild soap and water, dry, and apply topical antibiotic and a Band-Aid or 2nd Skin.

- Update tetanus shot every ten years.

PROPER TOENAIL CUTTING

- Cut toenails close and straight across to avoid bruising from shoes.

- Extend nail past corner to prevent ingrown toenails, and slightly round the end with an emery board.

SUPPLY KIT

Elastikon, nail nipper, emery board, orange stick, tweezers, sewing equipment, Band-Aids, 2nd Skin, padding (lambswool, gel pads, foam caps), moleskin, nonmedicated corn pads, bacitracin topical antibiotic, half-inch elastics in toe-shoe ribbons for Achilles tendonitis. For dance foot products, go to www.bunheads.com.

Turnout

Healthy turnout for dancing comes mainly from the bony shape of the ball and socket of your hip joint—normal, pigeon-toed, or duck-footed—which is predetermined at birth. (Note: Only a limited amount of turnout comes from below the knee, which should *never* be forced.) While most babies are born pigeon-toed, feet usually straighten out by the age of twelve. Normal hips have equal amounts of turn-in and turnout, creating poor rotation for ballet positions that require a 180-degree sideways motion using both feet. Dancers who remain pigeon-toed are unsuited for ballet, whereas duck-footed performers, who naturally have more turnout than turn-in, can easily assume these positions. However, dancers often find a way to get around their physical limitations, including asymmetries in the hips and knees.

The best way to eke out a few extra degrees of turnout involves strengthening the external rotator muscles in the buttocks through physical therapy or Pilates sessions and stretching the tight fibrous capsule surrounding the hip joint. The frog stretch is not recommended, says Katy Keller, clinical director of physical therapy at the Juilliard School and a therapist at NYCB. Although this stretch is a favorite among dancers, it often places excess stress on the knees, hips, and lower back, especially if you are asymmetrical. Instead, Keller prefers the pretzel stretch. Sit down with legs in front and place your right leg across your left knee. Use your left hand to pull up your foot as you push down your knee with your right hand. Stop at the point of discomfort and hold for thirty seconds, keeping your back straight. Repeat three times before switching legs.

Other ways to gain greater turnout are fraught with problems. For instance, let's say that you are a pigeon-toed dancer who has become a ballerina. What's going on? Chances are, you might have shallow hip sockets that allow your joints to sublux (or slip out), creating turnout at the expense of potential tears of the labrum or cartilage anchoring your hip joint. This is what happened to Mariah, a leading ballet dancer in a West Coast company who injured her hip while performing. An MRI with a hip coil revealed that she had shallow hip sockets with a labral tear that created pain in the groin. Fortunately, because the problem was caught early her injury responded to rest and rehabilitation without requiring surgery. It is important to treat labral tears because they may result in degenerative arthritis in the hip down the road. To prevent further injuries, Mariah is incorporating daily physical therapy exercises to strengthen her hip muscles and performs with a limited amount of turnout. In case you're wondering, her fans have never noticed!

Cutting corners to improve turnout by "screwing" your knee joints, which are meant to go up and down, *not* rotate, is another trap because it forces the feet to the side while the kneecaps face front. This situation is particularly dangerous for hypermobile dancers with weak thigh muscles and loose kneecaps that can pop in and out or dislocate, potentially tearing the cartilage or knee ligaments. Other tricks, like swaying your back and rolling in your feet and ankles, can create stress fractures and tendonitis, according to Dr. William Hamilton. A good teacher will never expect you to do this, so please don't do it to yourself.

Now that you have a better understanding of the unique characteristics of your body, the next step is to incorporate this information into good work habits.

The Work Habit Connection

Preparing your particular body to dance is a key ingredient of injury prevention and peak performance. Unfortunately, work habits like warming up, cooling down, and stretching often get overlooked, even by professional dancers who juggle an onslaught of daily classes, rehearsals, and performances. Creating a healthy balance between work and rest periods is also difficult but essential for high achievers. Lastly, dancers need to know how to care for minor aches and pains to reduce inflammation from intense exercise.

Why Dancers Need to Warm Up

Every type of athletic activity has its own pre-performance ritual. Dancers cross themselves three times, wish each other *merde,* and wear their lucky rhinestone earrings. These superstitious rituals, while reassuring, will not cut it after the age of twenty-one when the muscles begin to tighten. Consequently, whether you are a Rockette doing five shows a day or a classical ballet dancer performing Balanchine's fast-paced *Theme and Variations,* the most important ritual for today's versatile dancer is to warm up!

Surprisingly, this work habit is often overlooked, even in ballet. Yet dance students who warm up beginning in their early teens are less prone to injuries. The biggest mistake that dancers make is to use class to warm up rather than hone their technique, says physical therapist Marika Molnar. "Class shouldn't be the warmup for rehearsal or the rest of the day. You should actually try to come in a good half hour early and do the things that get you ready for class." While there is no consensus about the perfect warmup, all dancers can benefit by following these guidelines.

First, warmup exercises are intended to prepare your body for larger, more demanding movements, while decreasing the stress and strain on your muscles. This begins by increasing your body temperature and circulation with slow to moderate activity. Liz, a contemporary dancer, starts by gently prancing in place or using the stationary bike at a low intensity for ten minutes. She avoids jogging (unlike athletes), because it places undue stress on her turned-out knees and limbs. If her back is very tight, she will then add a series of slow back stretches to her usual abdominal sit-ups and curls. Abi and Megan use this time to strengthen their hypermobile ankles with a variety of exercises from physical therapy.

The next principle of warming up is to gradually increase your range of motion by doing simple moves for a limited period of time to open different body parts: for example, the pretzel exercise for turnout, or neck, shoulder, leg, and hip circles to loosen the joints. Avoid stretching major muscle groups until after you are warm (the ideal time is during the cooldown period). Instead, prepare your body for the steps to come. For instance, a ballet dancer can do a mini barre (minus grand pliés that stress the knees except in second position), whereas a modern dancer may prepare for a Merce Cunningham class by starting with simple exercises from his center. A Pilobolus dancer, who performs unique choreography that bears a strong resemblance to a living sculpture of entangled bodies, might incorporate a range of movements, such as yoga, Pilates, and Gyrokinesis, into her warmup.

Small isolated stretches prepare you for the kinds of movements you will use in class, such as getting some length in your calf for jumping. An easy exercise for elongating the calf is to stand in the parallel position and lean forward at a forty-five-degree angle with your hands on the barre and your knees straight, heels on the ground, for thirty to sixty seconds. Do up to five repetitions, then repeat the sequence with bent knees. A good warmup is also the time to mentally get into the zone for peak performance through focused breathing (not deep breaths) that help you concentrate, while bringing oxygen to your muscles. (Note: It is important to warm up cold muscles before any dance activity if you've been inactive for half an hour.)

Why Dancers Should Stretch Their Muscles

Two major injuries in dance are the pulled hamstring and the strained calf muscle, both of which result from tightness. Stretching after you are warm is the only way to increase your range of motion and prevent these injuries. However, you need to know when and how to safely elongate your muscles, while making adjustments for your body. For example, although flopping down into a side split is how dancers typically warm up, a study in a professional dance company shows that stretching cold muscles before class leads to more injuries over the course of a season. The other accepted (but inaccurate) belief about stretching is that more is better. Now, we know from studies in exercise physiology that stretching in your end range before you dance creates a smaller vertical jump, poorer balance, and impaired motor coordination. (Remember this when you go onstage!) A stretched-out muscle is a weaker muscle. If you push it too far, it can also become inflamed. It's best to save big stretches like splits and the large muscle groups for the cooldown period after dancing, with small gentle stretches before and during dance class.

While there are many different ways to stretch, three techniques are especially beneficial for dancers. These include:

STATIC STRETCHING, where you relax into a position to the point of mild discomfort (*not* pain) that diminishes over thirty seconds. This is the simplest way to increase your range of motion, as well as to recover during the cooldown period. The idea is to use another part of your body, a partner, or an external apparatus like the floor, the wall, or a belt to hold the stretch in place. An example would be the split. Inhale beforehand and exhale during a thirty- to sixty-second stretch to help your muscles relax. Repeat up to three times, several times a day, depending on your activity level. (Note: Bouncing can make the muscles reflexively tighten and tear.)

DYNAMIC STRETCHING that involves an evenly controlled swinging rhythm. This type of stretch will help prepare you for dance-specific skills, where you need the freedom to move your body. As usual, it is important to gradually increase the amplitude of a specific stretch, such as doing ten arm or leg circles in each direction, rather than immediately moving into an extreme stretch. Likewise, take care not to exceed your present range of motion when stretching any of your joints to prevent injuries. Certain cross-training workouts like Pilates and the Gyrotonic Expansion System incorporate these stretches into their strengthening programs.

PROPRIOCEPTIVE NEUROMUSCULAR FACILITATION (PNF) STRETCH-ING, often prescribed by physical therapists, takes advantage of the fact that gently tensing your muscles for ten seconds before letting go helps your body safely move into a longer stretch. This contract-relax technique also strengthens and stretches the muscle group. For example, to get a good hamstring stretch, lie down with one straight leg raised in the perpendicular neutral position at ninety degrees with a flexed foot in a static stretch. Take hold of the back of your thigh and tense the same or opposite muscle (the thigh or the hamstring) for ten seconds, then relax the muscle for three seconds before moving into a greater static stretch for another ten to fifteen seconds. Always relax the muscle for twenty seconds before repeating the movement; do it up to three times, then switch legs. It is also essential to take your body into account during stretching. If you have tight muscles, regular static stretching can increase your flexibility and protect your body from muscle pulls. "Loose-jointed dancers, however, often do better with foam rollers or tennis balls that put pressure directly into the muscle belly," says Katy Keller. "Being hypermobile makes it difficult to stretch the muscles because you just sink down into the joint when you try to stretch the whole leg." As always, pain is a sign that you have gone too far.

Finally, it is more effective to stretch one muscle group at a time like the hamstrings, while stabilizing the surrounding joints. This is preferable to standing and hanging over your leg at the barre, which stretches the back of your neck, upper back, and lower back across the buttocks and down your leg. Dancers also make the mistake of stretching tight areas in the direction they are used to moving, such as turning out their limbs. Yet stretching in the opposite direction (turn-in) will help release tightness. For specific exercises, it's best to have a physical therapist help you devise a stretching program that suits your body. You can also check out the reading material in Appendix A.

Why Dancers Need to Cool Down After Exercise

Although most dancers excel in terms of their work ethic, discipline, and single-minded approach to technique, they aren't into cool—at least when it comes to cooling down after exercise. Instead, nine times out of ten they take off from dancing ASAP to walk their dogs, hang out with their friends, or answer their e-mails into the wee hours of the night. Of course, you could be the exception by putting your physical needs first.

Cooling down is just as important as warming up. Besides helping to reduce delayed muscle tension and soreness the following day, cooling down after class, rehearsals, and performances helps your body calm down, especially after a late-night performance. Former NYCB corps dancer Carrie Lee Riggins says, "I have moments [after dancing] when my legs are so electrified that I have a hard time sleeping." A slow cooldown can help relax both mind and body. Here's why it works.

A cooldown period begins by simply walking around to help your heart rate slow down, thereby decreasing circulation and body temperature. You can then spend a total of ten to fifteen minutes stretching the large muscle groups, such as the calves, thighs, hamstrings, hips, and back. NYCB dancers often begin by standing on a slanted plywood stretch box built by the stagehands, with toes up and heels down at a twenty- to twenty-five-degree angle to stretch their Achilles tendon. You can do the same by propping the balls of your feet on the bottom rung of a dance barre and letting your heels sink down. This significantly reduces the chance of Achilles tendonitis in all types of healthy dancers, with one notable exception. According to podiatrist Thomas Novella, it can have a negative impact on muscle tone in performers with a high arch and tight calves who work in high heels. In this case, the only time to stretch would be if you had to switch from heels to flat feet. "It helps to stretch a few weeks ahead of time," he says, so "you don't set yourself up for problems, such as Achilles tendonitis and arch strains."

Addressing sore muscles during a cooldown is also important. As the heart rate slows down, the blood and fluids tend to pool in the soft tissues. Consequently, it always helps to take off your shoes, lie down, and end with your feet propped up on the wall to reduce swelling and inflammation. You may also want to add an ice pack under your clothes to any injured parts of your body if you plan to spend a (quiet) night on the town. Meanwhile, try to listen to your body for warning signals, like pain or excessive tightness from overstretching. A dance medicine specialist, such as a physical therapist or athletic trainer, can guide you in the right direction by ensuring proper technique for complicated stretches.

How to Use Periodization to Pace Yourself

All dancers have to juggle different work schedules, depending on their rank, technical obligations, and injury status. For example, if you are a leading male dancer in a ballet company who's cast primarily in partnering roles, your workload may be sporadic, whereas a colleague with a different set of skills might have multiple rehearsals and be onstage five times a week. In contrast, musical theater dancers in long-running shows often have free days but face the grind of doing the same performance over and over. Meanwhile, dance students' schedules vary according to whether they're engaged in an intense training program or preparing for a recital, while injured dancers in rehab are trying to regain health. Given these unique circumstances, how do you know when to take on extra classes or cross-train? The following guidelines derived from sports medicine can help you tailor your workload to your particular circumstances.

The concept of pacing, known as periodization, was developed in the USSR and former eastern bloc countries to enhance athletic performance. The goal is to divide each period of the year into phases with a different focus and training program. This helps to prevent symptoms related to overtraining (or burnout) that can impair your technique, tighten your muscles, and even cause you to lose your desire to dance. If you are experiencing any of these symptoms, your first impulse may be to work harder. Please don't! Rest, not dancing, is the only remedy. Optimizing performance means "planning out your entire year in advance," says Marika Molnar, "by alternating heavy workout periods with lighter workloads and rest breaks."

1. Do not dance yourself into shape after taking time off from exercise. Our research at NYCB found that this approach was a setup for injuries. Instead, know that all dancers begin to lose some technique after a two-week break, and that it can take up to six weeks to dance full-out after a break (except for children). The safest approach is to address residual tightness or weakness stemming from a prior injury, followed by several weeks of general

activities like cross-training. For example, Abi Stafford started back after her ankle surgery by doing rehab, the stationary bike for stamina, and Pilates exercises to gain strength and flexibility. She then moved on to adult beginner's ballet classes, where she slowly regained her ability to dance. A modern dancer like Leslie, who had a torn meniscus in her knee, benefited from the same methodical approach. Healthy dancers in every technique can return to more advanced classes after a break, as long as they ease back into a more rigorous routine.

2. All dancers need to give their bodies rest periods to recover from intense exercise. A freelance dancer who has just undergone back-to-back rehearsals and performances should not jump back into multiple classes and cross-training. Dancer Jenifer Ringer also makes adjustments within the confines of a company repertoire. "I definitely take one day off a week during the season and try to get ten hours of sleep at night by not setting my alarm, then taking a later class if possible." Power naps, while better than nothing, do not involve the deep stages of sleep that foster healing and recovery from exercise. In fact, the need for a nap is a sign of sleep deprivation. A vacation is the best way to recover from too much work, although shorter breaks are more suitable as you get older. Jenifer, who is in her thirties, believes in taking a good vacation once a year before easing back into class: "A full two weeks off for my body and mind. I find if I don't do it, I really suffer for it later." If you are a professional dancer, please don't fill up all your vacation time with extra gigs. Children under the age of twelve also need to take the summer off while remaining active outside of dance class. Dr. William Hamilton advises taking a summer program between the ages of twelve and eighteen, followed by two weeks off for normal fun activities, then two more weeks to slowly get back into shape.

3. After you've taken a break and gotten back into shape through cross-training, be sure to return to dance classes slowly. For example, you could follow modern dancer Jeremy's approach by taking an advanced class but spacing it out three times a week. Or you could model yourself after ballerina Jenifer Ringer by

taking the barre and adding a combination in the center every day. Then, there is Charles, a musical theater dancer who bypasses both the difficulty and duration of dance class in favor of frequency, taking five easy adult beginner's dance classes a week. If you are a dance student preparing for an intensive training program, slowly increase the number of dance classes every few days until you are ready to take on a rigorous schedule of three to four dance classes per day, often with extra rehearsals! Back off from cross-training during this time.

How to Take Care of Inflammation and Pain from Dancing

It is not unusual to experience physical discomfort after a hard workout. The important part is to deal with it. Whether the discomfort hits you right away or twenty-four hours later, you can relieve your discomfort by decreasing blood flow that leads to swelling, pain, inflammation, and damage to the soft tissues—even if you have to strap on a package of frozen peas with a cloth cover to prevent frostbite under your evening dress. (An acute injury, such as a sprained ankle, also responds to ice but requires an immediate visit to an orthopedist or physical therapist.) Here are basic tips to care for minor aches or pains.

Rest, ice, compression, and elevation (RICE) are beneficial during the first twenty-four to forty-eight hours following an injury. Rest minimizes bleeding and swelling, while ice decreases blood flow and helps to control pain. (Use a bag of ice or frozen peas wrapped in a moist towel for fifteen minutes on and off every two hours, several times a day.) An Ace bandage protects the area with gentle compression to control swelling. Elevation ("toes above the nose") works in tandem with these other modalities to lessen the initial effects of the injury.

After forty-eight hours, apply a moist heating pad (do not moisten a dry one) or alternate between heat and ice (fifteen minutes each) for thirty minutes every two hours. This promotes circulation and speeds up the healing process. If your goal is to reduce swelling, end with ice. Otherwise, end with heat to warm up for exercise. While ice minimizes inflammation and pain after dancing, avoid using it on the front of the hip. Not only are the joint structures too deep to respond, you can damage the femoral nerve that lies close to the surface at the crease of the hip and affect the movement of the quadriceps.

Meanwhile, restorative techniques such as massages, saunas, and whirlpools after the first day or two are additional ways to relieve the physical stress and pain of minor injuries. NYCB principal dancer Wendy Whelan uses acupuncture and massage on a weekly basis "to release the tension in my body from performing." The key is to pay attention to how you feel and use the modalities that work best for you. While dancers are expert at tuning out aches and pains, it is important not to ignore the normal pain you will inevitably experience at some point in your dancing career. This rule applies to serious students, professional dancers, and aspiring professionals. If an injury has occurred (i.e., you can't dance for three to five days), your company or dance school may benefit from using NYCB's injury reentry form to ease you back to dancing (Appendix F). This form requires that you and an orthopedist or physical therapist make periodic updates regarding your physical status. Examples include being able to jump, do pointe work, and return to your previous roles or level of training.

What about anti-inflammatory medications? There is a right way and a wrong way to use NSAIDs (nonsteroidal anti-inflammatory drugs such as ibuprofen). They are useful during the acute phase of a minor injury to reduce pain and swelling. However, you should not use them on a daily basis as painkillers because they slow down the healing process and may mask more serious injuries. These medicines also have some serious side effects, such as stomach ulcers and kidney failure associated with dehydration.

Behind the glamour and grace, dancers are hard-working dedicated professionals whose personal ideals often make it difficult to settle for anything less than perfection. However, the more you know about and practice healthy work habits throughout the year, the more you will achieve—individually and professionally.

To succeed, you need to understand your body type while setting aside time for healthy work habits. It also helps to plan out your year in advance, if possible, to avoid overtraining injuries. Similarly, while cross-training is highly beneficial, it only pays off if you do it during down periods, rather than adding it onto a busy schedule. TLC is equally important. Massages, along with the restorative powers of sleep, which releases human growth hormone to repair damaged tissues, do wonders. Wendy Whelan admits, "I never knew how valuable sleep was for healing until I was injured. It relaxes me to get ten hours a night." Lastly, ease back into dancing after a break. Your body will thank you!

SIX

Cross-Training Activities

*I really enjoy cross-training. It makes me feel more energetic and helps
so much with my overall strength.*

—ABI STAFFORD, NYCB principal

Cross-training is the new buzzword for today's serious dancer. Besides helping you nail more athletic choreography, it also reduces fatigue and injuries while improving the muscular shape of your body—that is, if you know what to do! Picking specific workouts and adding them to your dance schedule can be confusing, especially when the wrong match leaves you with bulkier muscles or a bad case of burnout. This chapter describes how to create an overall fitness program that works for you.

Why isn't dance class enough? While regular class is essential to excel in a specific dance technique, it bypasses certain muscle groups, and it does not raise your heart rate sufficiently. In fact, 85 percent of technique class is not up to the stamina required to perform onstage. The constant repetition of dance steps also stresses vulnerable areas of the body associated with teenage growth spurts, prior injuries, and your physique (for example, being tight- or loose-jointed). Thus, the value of an individualized cross-training program is twofold:

1. It improves your general level of fitness according to essential physical parameters (strength, flexibility, and aerobic capacity).

2. It compensates for specific areas of vulnerability after the age of twelve when dance training becomes more intense.

LEFT (Abi Stafford in George Balanchine's *The Nutcracker*)

Still, cross-training is only effective if the workouts complement your dance schedule. While nonathletes can cross-train year-round to spice up their fitness program and prevent pain by alternating routines, dancers who add it onto a new training program or during a busy work period are significantly more prone to overuse injuries. This happened to sixteen-year-old Jason, whose intensive summer dance program introduced an hour of cross-training on top of a full day of classes and rehearsals. By the end of the month, he had developed a bad case of tendonitis, much to his dismay, and missed the final dance recital. The key to cross-training is to know what to do, when to do it, and how to find qualified instructors. The best time is to use it to get in shape or recover from an injury.

Cross-Training: Maximizing Your Dance Potential

The idea behind cross-training is that you use different routines to create a total body workout that increases endurance, strength, and flexibility, rather than focusing on only one of these components. In addition, because the body requires twelve to twenty-four hours to benefit from a workout, there are two ways to proceed. You can do two or more workouts on the same day (for example, aerobics, weight lifting, and stretching), followed by a free day. Or you can alternate a harder day (such as thirty minutes of interval training on the elliptical machine) with an easier day (like a Pilates session). According to Marika Molnar, professional dancers who need to prepare for late-night performances may choose to work out in the morning and the evening to get into shape.

Expert supervision with certain workouts like Pilates is essential to ensure that you use the correct muscles without getting injured. Contact information for each of the major programs in this chapter is provided in Appendix A. Still, when in doubt, ask about a teacher's credentials. It takes several hundred hours of teacher training to understand how to modify exercises for individual students. An experienced teacher is someone who can take your anatomy, injuries, and emotional makeup into account and make suggestions specifically for you.

Meanwhile, please avoid power sessions with even the most experienced teachers, whether the focus is on exhausting routines, sweltering heat, or extreme positions. Although it may seem as if you are getting a better workout, the point of cross-training is to enhance your fitness level without adding undue stress to your body. Needless to say, the floor also needs to be resilient if you are doing impact exercises, such as jumping.

What Constitutes a Good Workout?

Regardless of the type of activity, a solid program eases you into a routine, beginning with a slow five- to ten-minute warmup that gradually progresses into more evolved exercises, followed by the same amount of time cooling down. This approach protects you from the initial shock associated with any new activity. To help you progress, a program should also challenge your body by varying the content, intensity, and timing of exercises. Known as the overload principle, this method prevents your body from adapting to any one routine and becoming complacent. Here is how cross-training works.

Tip

Exercises that teach you to isolate specific muscles rather than gripping a whole area like the buttocks enhance the fluidity of dance movements.

Aerobic Conditioning

Most people know that cardiovascular fitness is good for the heart. Unfortunately, few dancers realize that it also helps them to perform for longer periods by reducing the buildup of lactic acid (or lactate), which causes a burning sensation and muscle fatigue. Dancing generally involves rapid bursts of high-intensity exercise that is time-limited, because your energy comes from the muscles' carbohydrate or glycogen stores, *not* oxygen. Hence, the term *anaerobic* ("without air") is used to describe dance. Technique class will not prepare you to work for an extended performance of Twyla Tharp's nonstop choreography, for instance, *In the Upper Room*.

An aerobically fit dancer, in contrast, has a definite advantage. First, this form of exercise helps your body tap your carbohydrate stores more efficiently during sudden dance movements. It also conditions the heart to pump more oxygen to the working muscles. This can mean the difference between your heart rate beginning to return to normal within sixty seconds after a taxing variation and heavy panting for five minutes in the wings. This is true for all dancers, but especially if you are muscular with more fast-twitch muscle fibers that lack endurance. The fact that aerobic exercise also increases the diameter of the less bulky fast-twitch type A fibers, giving you a sleeker look, is an added bonus. Chapter 8 describes how all dancers can use endurance workouts to safely manage their weight. Still, the challenge is to know which workouts to choose, as well as the duration and intensity to get the best results.

The most straightforward approach is to do something that you enjoy, like the treadmill, and build up to a thirty-minute routine three times a week. The simplest, albeit less precise, way to gauge if your heart rate is sufficiently elevated while exercising is the talk test: You can talk but not sing or hold a conversation. You will definitely see an improvement in your stamina through regular exercise.

To achieve peak condition follow in the footsteps of Stella, a talented contemporary dancer. Knowing from past experience that many aerobic workouts place extra stress on the joints, she chooses to use the elliptical machine. This piece of gym equipment exercises both the upper and lower body for a great aerobic workout, while minimizing the physical impact on your joints. It's also an excellent way to burn fat. In contrast, high-impact activities where you're pounding the ground, like jogging or jumping rope, can cause overuse injuries, such as tendonitis. Other aerobic exercises can be problematic for different reasons, says Marika Molnar. The following list of common workouts gives you an idea of the potential negative repercussions for dancers.

- Riding the stationary bike with high resistance (10 mph or more) can create bulk and back strain.

- Spinning on a stationary bike with no resistance can strain the kneecaps.

- Swimming in cold water can increase appetite.

- Jogging can strain the foot, ankle, and knee, especially with turnout.

- Power walking can place stress on the hips.

- Climbing stairs can exacerbate bad backs.

- Jumping rope can stress all the joints of the lower body.

Some dancers can do these activities without problems. For example, NYCB principal Yvonne Borree loves swimming, joking: "My friends say I look like a swan on the kickboard." Abi Stafford uses the stationary bike with moderate resistance (less than 10 mph). For dancers who use the bicycle and need to reduce strain on the lower back, consider working on the recumbent bike with an armchair-type design. However, if you do develop any untoward effects from an aerobic activity, please switch to a different workout.

In Stella's case, she's satisfied with the elliptical machine. Her goal is to develop an aerobic foundation by working at 75 percent of her maximum heart rate (MHR) three times a week for thirty minutes over the next two weeks. This number will vary, depending on your age and gender (see box on the next page). Stella programs the machine at her gym to monitor her target heart rate as a twenty-year-old woman: 154 beats per minute. Of course, Stella can check her pulse by following the procedure in the box, or order a sports bra with a built-in heart monitor and a stopwatch at www.numetrex.com.

The next step for Stella is to gradually replace two of her steady routines with interval training, alternating a two-minute high-intensity workout at 90 percent MHR (185 bpm) with a two-minute moderate rest period of 65 percent MHR (134 bpm). This type of

% Maximum Heart Rate (MHR)

Subtract age from 226 for women and 220 for men. Multiply this number by a specific percentile to get your target heart rate. (For example, to calculate 75 percent MHR, multiply by 0.75.)

Count Your Heart Rate

Press three middle fingers on the wrist of the other hand beneath base of the thumb. Count the number of beats for ten seconds watching the second hand on a clock and multiply by six to determine beats per minute (bpm).

---

training, which mimics dancing, helps her heart rate drop even more quickly after a burst of intense activity while providing more power for strength and endurance.

The last form of conditioning involves sprinting, which is not really aerobic but helps build even more stamina for three-minute dance variations and other athletic choreography. It is one way to move from an aerobic foundation (continuous) and power (interval) to recovering even faster from high-intensity bouts (sprinting). This activity alternates thirty seconds of working to your absolute limit in any workout with ninety seconds where you stop and rest. Unfortunately, this isn't the right activity for Stella's naturally muscular body. A single bout of sprinting causes the body to release significant amounts of human growth hormone, which remains elevated for as much as two hours. The good news is that underdeveloped dancers can use three twenty-minute weekly sessions of sprinting to increase muscle mass. Just ease into it.

In summary, for most dancers it is sufficient to lay a sound aerobic foundation with continuous training three times per week for thirty minutes at a moderate level of intensity (75 percent of maximum heart rate). The choice of exercise depends on your schedule, motivation, and physical needs. As with all cross-training (endurance, strength, and flexibility), it will take at least six weeks to get into peak condition.

Strength Training

The other part of the picture is strengthening your muscles to help you move more easily without unnecessary effort, while maintaining your speed and range of motion. Body type will obviously come into play, as a loose-jointed dancer will benefit from different exercises than one who tends to be tight. Rehabilitating prior injuries is equally crucial, as Megan LeCrone discovered when she sprained her ankle for the second time after joining the company. A physical assessment by a dance medicine specialist, such as a physical therapist, can give you instant feedback about an appropriate exercise program by using the fitness screening at the end of this book. For example, a number of NYCB dancers have discovered that they had unrecognized weaknesses and muscle imbalances or needed to strengthen one group of muscles to work better with another group.

At the same time, the most important aspect of a cross-training program (apart from a sprung floor and a good instructor) is a balance of stretching and strengthening. Although it might seem counterintuitive, each time you perform an exercise to strengthen a muscle, you also shorten it. Stretching is necessary to counteract this response. While dancers can do this on their own, Pilates and the Gyrotonic Expansion System cover both aspects of conditioning in a complete way. These programs address key areas like the abdominals, pelvis, and back (the core muscles), which support the spine, and the lower body, with particular emphasis on the foot and ankle.

They also tap into slow-twitch muscle fibers, which do not create extra bulk, according to exercise physiologist Dr. Mathew Wyon. Stella, our contemporary dancer, was happy to hear this. Her gynecologist had advised her to start a weight-lifting program to increase her bone density, which was slightly below normal because of primary amenorrhea (menarche after age fifteen). This menstrual problem arose from years of fruitless dieting to streamline her muscular build. It is reassuring to know that she can use light weights to help her bones, as well as strengthen her body, without jeopardizing her leaner look. Even better, she can eat three healthy meals plus snacks with some helpful guidance. She sought a referral from the American Dietetic Association (www.eatright.org) for a sports nutritionist in her area. Follow-up phone interviews allowed her to identify one who worked with dancers.

Male dancers often need to build muscle mass for partnering, as well as for aesthetics. Julian, who hopes to get hired for the annual Radio City Christmas Spectacular, uses his local gym to get access to dumbbells and heavy weights. He learns to stress various muscle groups, such as his upper body and the core muscles that protect his back, under the supervision of a personal trainer. While everyone has a different starting point, the goal is to increase the amount of weight lifted with each additional set. Dr. Lawrence DeMann from NYCB's medical team offers the following example: "Let's say for instance, you lift a weight of fifty pounds and you can do that ten times. By the time you get to ten it's a little bit hard. The next set, you add ten more pounds, so you really can't do ten repetitions. You're struggling to do just eight. Then, the next set you add another ten pounds, so you're now lifting seventy pounds and you're struggling to do even five or six repetitions."

Muscle gain requires that you fatigue as many muscle fibers as possible, because they strengthen and grow in response to stress. For the record, this does not mean overtraining, which is associated with impaired performance. Aim to lift weights four times a week with a day off between sessions. If you do not see improvement, cut back on regular aerobic exercise, as this workout burns extra calories in addition to speeding up your metabolism. Sprinting will help you consolidate your gains.

Regular strength training should be done at least twice a week. We do not recommend that teenage dancers use heavy weights during periods of rapid growth. It is also important to have appropriate supervision. A personal trainer can help you develop a fitness program at your gym. Athletic trainers and physical therapists, in contrast, focus on injury rehabilitation and prevention.

Range of Motion Training

Stretching is an important part of maintaining your natural flexibility, which tends to decrease with age. However, there are periods when you need to back off, like adolescent growth spurts, when you temporarily lose flexibility as your bones shoot up while your muscles, ligaments, and tendons lag behind. Carol is a sixteen-year-old ballet student who thought she was losing her talent when she grew almost four inches in a year. Rather than back off, she would sit in a side split for an hour in front of the television until she eventually tore some muscle fibers in her adductors (the muscles on the inside of the thigh). This is a serious injury because the damage creates a tight band of scar tissue, which she now has to deal with in physical therapy.

The best time to stretch is when you are warm, preferably after dance class as part of cooling down. Yet be aware that your muscles are also fatigued, so take it easy by following the instructions for static stretching in Chapter 5. In addition, stretching is not a competition between you and the most loose-jointed dancer in your class. Instead, keep the focus on your own needs and capabilities, stretching each of your major muscle groups to the point of mild discomfort, knowing it's not how hard you stretch but how often.

There are also distinct disadvantages to long stretches (more than thirty seconds) before you dance. A study in *Medicine & Science in Sports & Exercise* by Canadian researchers at the Memorial University of Newfoundland shows that students who warm up on the stationary bike for five minutes and stretch their legs to the point of discomfort, maintaining three different static stretches for forty-five seconds each, do not do well. This is true even though they only repeat the stretch three times, with fifteen-second rest breaks. The results indicate a significant decrease in their balance, reaction time, and movement time, compared to a group that did not stretch and rested after cycling. The authors speculated that stretching may change muscle compliance or the tendency to yield.

Thus, stretching is a double-edged sword. Dancers must lengthen their muscles to avoid pulls and tears due to tightness. However, it is necessary to do it correctly by following general guidelines for stretching different muscles. For example, it is important to stretch the hamstrings and the quadriceps, which are your primary muscles for locomotion. Called *antagonistic muscles* because they either raise the knee up or curl the leg back, they tend to be extremely unbalanced in terms of strength. By properly stretching the weaker hamstrings, you are less likely to overload them with your more powerful quadriceps. It is also crucial to stretch the calves, the iliotibial band along the outside of the thigh, hip flexors, chest, and front of the shoulders. For details, check out *Stretching* by B. Anderson (details are in Appendix A).

Choosing a Strengthening and Stretching Program

Because there are so many programs to choose from, the pressure to find the right one can feel overwhelming. By far, the most popular conditioning programs among dancers are Pilates, Gyrotonic, and yoga. All three are considered mind-body methods, because of the high level of mental concentration required. They also emphasize breathing, postural alignment, balance, coordination, and imagery (visualizing your spine as a strand of pearls as you roll back down from the sitting position to the floor, for example). Some performers focus on a couple of different programs; others switch from one to another. To see improvement, you need to take two to three classes a week under the guidance of an experienced teacher.

Pilates

This unique workout is an excellent start-up program for most beginners because it works in a linear progression, with both sides of the body moving in unison. It is also a favorite among professional dancers like Abi Stafford, who continued to use it after her ankle surgery to retain extra strength and flexibility. Other dancers, like eighteen-year-old Karen, find it quite helpful during their growth spurts as a way to stay in shape, rather than pushing too hard in dance class. The Pilates technique also allows ballet dancers to exercise in their position of function (that is, turned out).

Devised by German gymnast Joseph Pilates in the 1920s, this program was a well-kept secret in the dance world long before Hollywood discovered it in the mid-1980s as a way to develop an ultratoned body—without having to go for the burn. Pilates (pronounced pul-LAH-tees) appears deceptively easy. It provides incredible core strength in the abdominals and lower torso, the "powerhouse" of the body and the foundation for every movement, with a combination of yoga and calisthenics. Deep concentration and rhythmic breathing are emphasized. Gentle stretching accompanies each strengthening exercise.

The two main components of Pilates exercises are matwork, involving a series of calisthenic exercises performed on a padded mat, and machines, using springs, ropes, slings, and pulleys for additional resistance. Although the matwork is often taught separately today at gyms, you will achieve the best results if you practice both in one session. The machines ease you into some of the more complex movements, taking you to a whole new level, where you work on all the muscle groups. Color-coded springs make it easy to adjust the level of resistance, which can change the difficulty of the exercise. This makes it easier to go through a full range of motion, such as leg circles, where you both stretch and strengthen the limbs.

Pilates instructor Deanne Lay believes in the many benefits of this type of conditioning. However, she says, "These can be outweighed if your placement is off. It needs to be taught correctly from the beginning, so that you learn the right movement patterns." A good example is the focus on the "neutral spine" (the natural arch under the lower back), which is based on medical knowledge over the last decade due, in large part, to input from physical therapists who use Pilates during rehab. Marika Molnar explains: "The danger of the flat back is that it puts a lot of pressure on the lower discs and joints. With the neutral spine, you're in a better place to work your deep abdominals that stabilize the back and prevent injuries." To locate a qualified practitioner, contact the Pilates Method Alliance.

Gyrotonic

Another popular conditioning program is Juliu Horvath's Gyrotonic Expansion System, which uses many of the same principles as Pilates. In fact, certain dancers find that these conditioning programs complement each other. The main difference with Gyrotonic is that the machines are inspired by Horvath's deep interest in yoga. As a former ballet dancer in Romania, he prefers to work three-dimensionally on the body in circular, spiraling movements that span multiple joints and also allow for turnout. The result is that the left and right sides of the body work independently at the same time, using pulleys that are connected to separate weight sources. Dancer Wendy Whelan prefers using this asymmetrical approach because of her pronounced scoliosis; she found that Pilates, which worked both sides in unison, was painful.

As with Pilates, the origin for all movements in Gyrotonic stems from the core abdominals. In addition to working both sides independently, you focus on the upper and lower body. Some dancers find this dual emphasis places undue stress on vulnerable areas. Others, like Wendy and Megan LeCrone, who also switched from Pilates to Gyrotonic, find that the extra focus on movement is a liberating experience. "It helped me to know when to use my strength and when not to," Megan says. "I felt a greater awareness about my body while I was moving." Yet the ultimate test is how a program or specific exercise feels to you, regardless of what works for someone else. If your back starts to hurt, for example, it's time to have a discussion with your teacher about eliminating exercises or changing your approach. Both teacher and student need to be open to feedback in a healthy cross-training program.

It is best to ease into a new routine. In this case, the floor version of Gyrotonic without machines is called Gyrokinesis, which simulates movements on the machine on your back, stomach, and in seated positions. Michelle, a twenty-seven-year-old musical theater dancer, likes it because it focuses on stretching and strengthening movements, frees up her joints, and improves coordination. She also uses some of the movements to warm up for dance class and performances, whereas Abi uses Pilates matwork. For referrals, check out Juliu Horvath's studio information on the general Gyrotonic Web site at www.gyrotonic.com.

Yoga

In India the Sanskrit word *yoga* refers to bringing mind, body, and spirit together as a way to enlightenment. It's up to you to choose whether to make it a way of life or simply a form of exercise. The traditional form, called hatha yoga, has become associated with the asanas, or postures, considered to be fitness exercises for many people in the West. Traditional yoga is a set of sequences, including breathing exercises, that improve strength, flexibility, and physical well-being. Megan, who has struggled with perfectionism, says, "I now do breathing exercises from yoga before a performance. You have all that adrenaline, knowing you have to go onstage. But instead of playing with my pointe shoes, costume, and headpiece, I do ten deep breaths in and out. I use yoga to calm down."

Hilary Cartwright teaches Yoga for Dancers, a class that also emphasizes breathing and is especially suited for performers (see www.hilarycartwright.com). The class doesn't begin with extreme positions, but builds up to more difficult movements like a dance class. Some steps are also done in a mini turned-out position, because it is more dancer-friendly than standing with the feet parallel. "It's not about how big the back bend is or how deep the stretch," says NYCB corps dancer Dena Abergel, "but strengthening your core muscles to create fluid movement." It isn't power yoga, which often forces dancers into extreme positions that may create injuries. While Yoga for Dancers is mainly available in New York City, traditional hatha yoga with an experienced teacher is a safe and reliable option for dancers outside of New York. Find out more about your yoga options by checking out the yoga Web sites featured in Appendix A.

Weight Training

As we have already learned, using weights is an essential element of building muscle strength. While it's a good idea to work out a program with professional guidance, these are a couple of examples of working your upper body. The goal for each of the following exercises is three sets of ten slow repetitions, three times per week. It's always important when standing to relax the knees and contract the abdominals to support your spine. Pick a manageable but challenging weight to avoid injury.

For example, Melissa, an aspiring tap dancer, uses a three-pound weight in each hand to do bicep curls, holding her arms straight in front of her with palms facing the ceiling, shoulder-width apart and perpendicular to the floor. She then curls her arms toward her chest and lengthens them back out for her set repetitions. Next, she works on her deltoids (the front, side, and back of the shoulders), extending her arms straight in front, palms facing each other at shoulder height. She holds them there for a moment and slowly lowers her arms back down to her side for each set. Melissa does the same exercise taking her arms out to the side up to shoulder height with palms facing down before lowering them to her start position. She completes the last deltoid exercise by raising her arms straight back aligned with the shoulder joint, going only as high as she can before bringing them back down. (Note: If you don't have dumbbells, you can use ankle weights instead.) A professional, such as a Pilates instructor or a personal trainer, can provide a full set of upper-body exercises.

Impediments to Cross-Training

By now, I hope that the benefits of improving strength, flexibility, and aerobic capacity are evident in terms of their positive impact on your dancing. So what holds many dancers back from adding them to their routine? I'm afraid some of it has to do with the difficulty of changing ingrained habits even if it helps you get to the next level in your career. Traditionally, dancers have always relied on class to prepare them for the stage. Many of their teachers still believe that hard work is sufficient, since they relied on class as well. There is also the idea that dancers are artists, not athletes. Yet change is in the air. Many schools have begun to add cross-training to their curriculum, breeding a new generation of savvy dancers who are comfortable going to the gym or seeking out other ways to improve their overall fitness. Thus, while the more seasoned professionals may be sticking to their old routines—at least until they get injured—young dancers are more open to change if it will help them achieve their goals.

At the same time, dancers need to use cross-training realistically in their professional life. Do more during the layoff to stay performance-ready, but cut back during the season. Abi Stafford agrees, saying, "I don't do a whole lot at the gym or Pilates when I'm performing because it's too much. But I miss it." It's fine to combine cross-training with daily technique classes if you feel up to it *and* your dance schedule does not exceed five hours per day. Otherwise, you may set yourself up for an overuse injury. In a survey of five hundred injury reports, 79 percent occurred after the fifth hour of dancing. A well-paced conditioning program can use cross-training in addition to dance classes for getting back into shape.

Getting Fit for Dance

Cross-training can help you in various situations both during and after the season or for an intense summer program. However, it works best when you are rested and need to get ready for a demanding dance schedule. Here is a case study of a professional dancer who used it to prepare for rehearsals and performances.

Amanda is a young modern dancer who has just returned from a long, tiring tour. She hopes to regain her energy over an eight-week break by sleeping ten hours a night and letting her mom prepare her favorite home-cooked meals. Two weeks go by before she even considers doing any kind of exercise. Fortunately, her company's physical therapist has provided helpful suggestions about easing back into dance. Amanda decides it's worth a try. This is only her first year as a professional dancer and she wants to return to the company in peak condition. Here is her program (see table).

The first two weeks of exercise (weeks 3 and 4 of her eight-week break) start off with three weekly sessions on the stationary bike. She stays within a moderate rate that's less than 10 mph, bringing her up to 75 percent of her maximum heart rate for thirty minutes. This provides an aerobic foundation. Amanda also adds two weekly Pilates sessions, focusing on core stability (abs, pelvis, and lower back) and motor control to establish correct alignment in preparation for more complex exercises that lie ahead.

The next two weeks (weeks 5 and 6) Amanda replaces one steady aerobic workout with one interval training routine where she alternates between 90 percent and 65 percent MHR. She adds simple arm and leg movements to her Pilates sessions, such as leg circles, while continuing to stabilize her core. This is also the time when she brings in one dance class, five days a week, omitting big jumps, partnering, and complex combinations until week 6 (see below).

The last two weeks (weeks 7 and 8) include one steady and two interval aerobic workouts, and two Pilates sessions with complex exercises, such as stabilizing the pelvis by raising it off the mat in a bridge while lying on her back, extending one leg out and in, with a repeat to the other side, and rolling down. She completes six weekly dance classes, working full-out. All of this helps her focus physically and mentally in preparation for going back to work.

Cross-Conditioning Program

NUMBER OF WORKOUTS PER WEEK

	CARDIO	PILATES	DANCE CLASS
WEEKS 1–2	———	———	———
WEEKS 3–4	3 steady heart rate	2 core stability	———
WEEK 5	2 steady +1 interval heart rate	2 core + extremities	5 w/o big steps/ jumps
WEEK 6	repeat	repeat	5+1 big step per class
WEEKS 7–8	1 steady +2 interval heart rate	2 core + complex moves	6 whole classes

In contrast to professional dancers, Joe is a student who plans to take a summer intensive in July and return to his old dance school in September. He will need to rest for at least two weeks in August. He can then alternate cross-training with a modified dance class in the third week, before gradually working up to five or six full dance classes in the last week prior to returning to his regular dance program.

Cross-training is proving to be beneficial for dancers in every genre, beginning in adolescence when most injuries first occur. However, you need to find the right workout, pace yourself according to your needs, and have proper guidance. It is equally important to enjoy your workouts and have fun. Remember, even adding a little more exercise at a time will really help your dancing.

SEVEN

Eating Right to Stay Fit

We work so hard as dancers that I actually worry about getting in enough food.

—YVONNE BORREE, NYCB principal

Smart eating habits are a necessary component of peak performance. Besides protecting your health, the right foods boost energy, improve stamina, strengthen bones, and speed up the healing process of dance injuries. Unfortunately, certain factors can interfere with making healthy choices, not the least of which is dieting. Many dancers worry about losing or gaining weight, which is why I have devoted all of Chapter 8 to this topic. This chapter covers the basics of sound nutrition, because all dancers need to know how to eat in a healthy way to fuel their bodies. Abi Stafford, who has been promoted to a principal after overcoming her long bout with injuries, agrees, saying, "My body has never felt better since I started eating a well-rounded diet and drinking lots of water."

It's no surprise that the nutritional requirements of dancers are unique compared to the general population: hence Yvonne Borree's concern about eating a sufficient amount of calories. After all, how many people perform an athletic dance repertoire that includes jazz, modern, ballet, and theater dance? To meet these demands, the International Association for Dance Medicine & Science has put out the "Nutrition Fact Sheet: Fueling the Dancer" available at www.iadms .org. The Dancer's Diet described in this chapter is similar with a few minor exceptions. Rather than using IADMS's formulas for calories based on weight and sex, dancers get to choose from ranges that are

LEFT (Yvonne Borree in George Balanchine's *Serenade*)

estimated to meet different energy needs for each gender during exercise, breaks, and injury status. Also, more emphasis is placed on protein because of its role in repairing stressed muscles and healing injuries. The final point of departure involves using a food diary to change your eating habits for the better.

Do's and Don'ts for the Dancer's Diet

The key to a healthy dancer's diet is to like what you eat, while knowing the benefits (and potential dangers) in different foods. Diana, a modern dance student, was understandably nervous about making her initial appointment with a nutritionist. While she knew that a diet of white bagels, gummy bears, and giant salads with low-calorie dressing wasn't the most balanced food plan for dance, Diana, being a true perfectionist, did not want to hear about what she was doing wrong. To her absolute astonishment, the nutritionist was nonjudgmental about her eating habits. She understood that their ability to work together depended on setting mutually agreed-upon goals, which included her food preferences. Diana learned that it was important to eat a variety of nutritious foods, with some fun foods on the side—including occasional gummy bears! In fact, in moderation, no food is off-limits. The key is to eat the right balance of calories, different food groups, micronutrients, and fluids. The Nutrition Fact Label on products will list the ingredients, as well as any added fat, sodium, or sugar. You can also find nutrition data for specific foods, fast-food restaurants, and meals on the Internet at www.thecaloriecounter.com.

If you decide, like Diana, to work with a nutritionist, be aware that many states do not require any particular training for a person to use this title. So choose an expert, such as a registered dietician (R.D.) who has had to pass a national exam, earn a bachelor's degree, and complete postgraduate training. The American Dietetic Association can provide you with an appropriate referral, at www.eatright.org. Remember, knowledge is power, especially if you want the strength and energy to dance.

Calories

The first question that every dancer needs to ask is, "Am I eating enough food?" An optimal dancer's diet rests on taking in sufficient calories. Apart from giving you enough energy, adequate amounts of food provide you with micronutrients (vitamins and minerals), which affect your growth and general health. Your resting metabolic rate alone burns roughly a minimum of 1,200 calories per day, so ingesting a lot more food is crucial to prevent your body from going into conservation mode, leading to a slower metabolism and menstrual irregularities. Eating a balanced diet with sufficient calories helps preserve muscle mass, prevent fatigue, illness, and injury—and keep you on top of your game. If you become injured, adequate food intake will speed up the healing process.

So how many calories do you need? Registered dietician Laura Pumillo, who works with all types of dancers under the auspices of NYCB's nutritionist, Joy Bauer, has established ranges, depending on your workload and injury status (see box). Obviously, you need to ingest more calories during heavy dancing, so aim for the higher numbers during the most intense work periods. Breaks require less energy. Still, it's absolutely fine to enjoy yourself and forget about calories during a vacation. If you are totally inactive because of an injury, you could gain weight from burning fewer calories. This is not the end of the world. However, if you want to avoid weight gain, aim for the lower number of calories during a total break from exercise. Diana learned to her surprise that diet foods are filled with hidden traps, including extra calories.

Dancers' Daily Caloric Needs

	FEMALE	MALE
ACTIVE	2000–2700	2200–3000
BREAKS	1800–2400	2000–2700
INJURED	1800	2000

Choose Your Food Groups

Now that you know about calories, the next step is to choose the correct percentage of each food group to create a balanced meal plan. In general, nutritionist Laura Pumillo believes that a dancer's diet should be composed of 55 to 60 percent carbohydrates, 15 to 20 percent protein, and 20 to 30 percent fat. These percentages fall within the ranges recommended by IADMS, with the exception of a slightly higher percentage of protein to maintain muscle mass and recover from dance injuries. Carbohydrates and fat are necessary for the production of hormones and the absorption of fat-soluble vitamins. All three food groups also provide energy for exercise, which is why it is good to mix and match.

Carbohydrates

This food group is the Big Daddy of energy for anaerobic exercise like dance. Yet, as with everything else in life, there are pluses and minuses. Some carbohydrates (for example, sugar) are throwaway calories that create a quick burst followed by a drop in energy, causing fatigue and hunger pangs. This happened to Diana when she gorged on gummy bears. Others (whole grains, fruits, and vegetables) are full of nutrients and fiber that fuel your body throughout the day. These so-called complex carbohydrates increase long-term energy for dancing. Be aware that muscle stores of carbohydrates are quickly used up in dance, making it crucial to eat adequate amounts at meals and snacks. About 300 grams per day is necessary for optimal dance performance.

In terms of starches and grains, the more they have been ground, milled, and stripped of their natural fiber, the faster the body digests them into sugar. Refined starches (any white grain product, like rice, bread, and pasta) can release large amounts of insulin, which is the fat storage hormone. Manufacturers have responded by adding back some fiber to traditional white flour starches, such as pasta. However, whole grains (milled in their entirety) are still the best, followed in descending order by cracked grains (cut into pieces), flaked or rolled grains (flattened kernels), and powdered grains (pulverized into flour). Diana discovered that even so-called healthy cereals might as well be in the candy section of the supermarket. Check out the fiber content on the nutution label and look for the word "whole." Rice cakes sound healthy, but they are actually low in fiber.

Tip

Pick breads with at least 2 grams of fiber per slice. Pasta should have 4 grams per two dry ounces. Cereals need 3 to 5 grams per cup.

Fruits and vegetables are full of vitamins, minerals, and fiber. They provide generous amounts of vitamin C, which protect you during periods of physical stress. Fruits are a great source of energy, plus their natural sweetness (whether fresh or dried) makes them a satisfying snack. Just watch out for the added sugar in yogurt and canned or frozen products, and try to avoid juices, which tend to be low in fiber and high in calories. One six-ounce glass of orange juice is OK, but a real orange is better. Diana didn't know that the most nutritious vegetables are dark green or yellow-orange, although variety is key. Certain produce will be more appetizing to you, depending on your taste. Rather than forcing yourself to eat something you hate because it's "good for you," find ways to add vegetables to dishes that you already enjoy.

Some dairy products, like milk and yogurt, also contain carbohydrates in the form of lactose (milk sugar) and possibly added simple sugars. A good example is low-fat frozen yogurt, which is a highly processed food often loaded with sugar, and therefore extra calories. Ideally, you should try to use fruit to sweeten most of your food. If, on occasion, you want to satisfy your sweet tooth, reach for the real thing. A chocolate chip cookie can hit the spot. Moderation, not abstinence, is the key. So limit sugar to less than 10 percent of your daily caloric intake and you'll be on the road to healthier eating habits. Even Diana found this acceptable.

Protein

Protein is another source of fuel for exercise, especially for endurance activities like riding the stationary bike. This food group helps repair muscle fibers, forms enzymes that boost metabolism, and maintains strong bones, so it is essential for dancers. Like fiber, it also sends a message to your brain that you are full. Aim for about 70 grams per day while keeping in mind that only some protein sources are "complete"—that is, they contain all essential amino acids vital for life that your body cannot make on its own.

Animal products, such as dairy (made from milk), meat, eggs, and poultry, are considered to be complete sources of protein, with important vitamins and minerals. Low-fat dairy products such as cheese and yogurt are terrific for bone health, especially when they are fortified with vitamin D to enhance calcium absorption. Red meat, in turn, helps build muscles and is rich in iron, which plays an important role in making red blood cells that prevent anemia. The B vitamins in red meat are also critical for energy production. Two to three servings a week are recommended, and a portion should be three to four ounces. A leading male dancer in musical theater now makes a point of getting sufficient protein. "I know you can get protein from beans, nuts, and other sources," he says. "Personally, I think it's good to have a piece of meat once in a while." Because many cuts of red meat are high in saturated fat, go lean with top round beef or pork tenderloin. The highest fat content is generally found in prime or choice cuts, rather than select cuts. Most restaurants offer prime cuts, so Diana makes a point of specifically asking for a select cut when she goes out to dinner. Skinless poultry is also a good choice.

Seafood contains high-quality protein, with essential nutrients, low saturated fat, and omega-3 fatty acids. These nutritional benefits contribute to a healthy heart and proper growth and development. Two portions a week, one from an oily fish low in mercury (for example, sardines, red snapper, and sablefish), are considered to be part of a well-balanced diet. Fresh tuna, which can be high in mercury, should be eaten once a month; canned chunk light tuna can be eaten once per week. Other fish that are low in mercury include shrimp, catfish, and salmon. (Wild, or Alaskan, salmon is also low in other contaminants.) Grilling or broiling fish allows the fat to drip off, unlike frying.

Vegetarians can use legumes, nuts, seeds, and fake meats like seitan (pronounced say-tan) made from wheat gluten for added protein. However, only soy products have all the essential amino acids on this list, although they are not recommended for anyone who is at risk for breast cancer or possible thyroid disorders. The good news is that you can combine foods with different amino acids, such as rice and beans, for a complete protein. These combinations can occur throughout the day (not necessarily within each meal), as long as the food is high in quality with sufficient calories. Vegans (those who do not consume any animal products) should seek nutritional counseling. While it's possible to get important nutrients from plant sources, it isn't simple—for example, iron isn't easily absorbed unless consumed with vitamin C. Be aware that iceberg lettuce has almost no nutrients, whereas romaine has the most, followed by green leaf, red leaf, and butterhead lettuce.

Fat

If you want to promote cell structure, insulate the layer around your nerves, produce hormones, and absorb fat-soluble vitamins, reach for fat—as long as it's the good, unsaturated kind. During exercise, the chief form of fat from any source stored in the body (as triglycerides) is broken down into fatty acids, producing energy for muscle contraction. This process also provides stamina for endurance activities that last over twenty minutes. Although this food group is high in calories, small amounts of fats and oils are important aspects of sound nutrition, from enhancing food satisfaction, taste, and texture to providing benefits to your heart. For example, omega-3 and omega-6 essential fatty acids cannot be made by the body. Instead, we need to get them from healthy vegetable oils (fish and lean meats are additional sources). Aim for a minimum of 40 grams of fat in your diet. Meanwhile, here are some guidelines.

First, avoid trans fats—partially hydrogenated fatty acids found in margarine and certain processed foods—as these raise your cardiovascular risk for heart disease. Besides increasing "bad" LDL cholesterol (low-density lipoproteins), which clogs up your arteries, trans fats lower the "good" HDL cholesterol (high-density lipoproteins), which clears away these deposits. That is just one of the nasty things trans fats do. In fact, they are so bad that New York City has set a national standard by adopting a municipal ban of all but tiny amounts of trans fat in restaurant food. Still, there are no safe amounts. Tropical oils like coconut, palm, and palm kernel, which are starting to replace trans fats, are saturated fats and are also injurious to your health. Diana learned that it's best to eat monounsaturated fats from olive and canola oil, nuts, seeds, and foods like avocados. Polyunsaturated fat from vegetable oils (corn, sesame, safflower, and sunflower) is also a healthy option. Saturated fats from red meat should still comprise only 10 percent of your fat intake.

Hydration

Did you know that lean muscle, blood, and even your brain contain about 70 percent water? In fact, water is one of the body's most vital ingredients for survival. An active male dancer needs about thirteen 8-ounce glasses of fluids per day, whereas female dancers require roughly nine cups. If you are flying at high altitudes, dancing more than usual, or sweating intensely you need more. Drinking water regulates body temperature, removes waste products (reducing constipation), helps detoxify the liver and kidneys, and transports oxygen and nutrients through the body. Water also dissolves vitamins and minerals. Other liquid options include 1 percent milk, sports drinks low in sugar, and fruit juice in moderation. (See "Hydration and Foods" section, on page 98.)

Caffeine and carbonated soft drinks, considered for many years to be a threat to healthy bones, have been somewhat exonerated, as long as you "drink your milk" or get sufficient calcium from other sources. Still, recent studies show that caffeine can be dehydrating above 575 mg, so avoid drinking two Starbucks grandes at 330 mg each. Sodas are also high in sugar. While there is no definitive research on the hazards of consuming diet sodas, Diana learned that the data suggest it may increase cravings, appetite, and the desire for sweets. Meanwhile, caffeine-containing "energy drinks" are a definite no-no in excess.

Besides making you feel anxious and jittery, they are dehydrating when consumed in large amounts. The American College of Sports Medicine has advised high school athletes to avoid them, and you should do the same.

Finally, it pays to address early symptoms of dehydration, such as dizziness, fuzzy thinking, minor cramps during exercise, and mild headaches. Abi Stafford agrees. "Anytime I feel a headache coming on or even if my muscles are sore or tired, I just drink water. That's all I need to feel better." Still, it's important to pace yourself with fluid intake and drink at least one half-cup of water every fifteen minutes during heavy exercise. After dance resist the urge to gulp down a quart of water, because this creates a false sense of security. While the color of your urine will look like you're hydrated (like lemonade, not apple juice), your body cannot process more than two cups of water an hour. Because vitamins can discolor your urine, the only way to tell if you're really hydrated is to measure its density and acidity. HydraTrend strips can provide an accurate reading when you compare the color to a chart (see www.uridynamics.com).

The last point to consider is overhydration. While drinking ahead of your thirst has always been the mantra to avoid dehydration, drinking too many fluids can be dangerous. How can you tell? If you feel ill—nauseated and groggy—and gain weight after exercise, you have gone overboard on fluids. Fortunately, this rarely happens to dancers (except in cases of extreme dieting), because they don't run three-hour marathons. Dancers would have to drink more than seventeen cups of total fluid for the day to become overhydrated.

Supplements

Unless you are skimping somewhere in your diet, you should be getting all of your nutrients from food. Still, IADMS recommends a daily multivitamin for insurance. Avoid single vitamins or minerals because megadoses can be toxic and lead to health problems (for example, liver disease from excessive amounts of niacin). Even energy drinks with extra B vitamins can result in a rapid heartbeat, numbness, and tingling in your hands and feet. The exception to this rule is calcium, which can protect the density in your bones. Dr. Michelle

Warren, an endocrinologist, feels strongly that all dancers (including men) should supplement their diet with 1,200 to 1,500 mg of calcium and 800 units of vitamin D to promote absorption. The extra magnesium and vitamin K in your multivitamin with minerals will also help your body absorb calcium. To find out the latest information about vitamins, supplements, and popular nutritional products from the leading provider in independent testing, you can become a member of Consumer Lab for a nominal fee (www.consumerlab.com).

Hydration and Foods: Before, During, and After Exercise

Combining nutrient-dense selections from each food group is a great way to ensure a high-performance meal plan. The challenge is to eat the right foods every three to four hours, beginning with breakfast and followed by a snack before and after dancing. It's also important to refuel throughout the day to store adequate amounts of carbohydrates in your muscles. Timing is important. Diana was surprised to learn that a light carbohydrate snack with some protein (for example, an apple with peanut butter) at least an hour prior to exercise increases circulating glucose levels, adding to the glycogen stored in her body. Remember, dancers need glycogen from high-fiber carbohydrates for energy, and protein causes the cells to open up and accept fuel. The combination of fiber and protein also stabilized her blood sugar. To get hydrated, she drank one to two cups of cold water (which is absorbed faster than warmer liquids) thirty minutes prior to dance class, while staying away from fluids that remained in her stomach for longer periods of time (such as milk and salty tomato juice).

After exercise, Diana refueled with a mixed snack, such as fruits and nuts. She also hydrated her body by drinking fluids for the next two to three hours, especially water. While carbonated drinks and large amounts of fruit juices may cause you to bloat, small quantities of orange juice with a high potassium content (300 mg) help replace what you have lost by sweating. Low-fat milk is also a good recovery drink, because of the mixture of carbohydrates and protein. Ideally, the most efficient way to keep the energy in your body flowing for endurance exercise and dancing is water along with a healthy mixed snack (an apple with low-fat cheese, a banana with peanut butter, raisins with plain yogurt, grapes with almonds, trail mix). Be aware that alcohol increases swelling after an injury.

Fueling Your Injured Body

Healthy eating can help prevent dance injuries. However, if you do become injured at some point, you may be like other dancers, including Diana, who tend to cut back on calories and fluids to prevent weight gain from lack of exercise. Please don't! While it's fine to reduce carbohydrates and fat and aim for the lowest number of healthy calories, you need to maintain an adequate amount of protein for recovery (70 or more grams). Megan LeCrone learned that she was low on protein while recovering from her injuries. Now she says, "I bring along foods like hard-boiled eggs," rather than heading for the vending machine at the theater. "You need to be conscious about what you put into your body," says Megan. "It's your instrument." Fluid intake to remove toxins away from the site of injury is equally crucial for injured dancers.

Food and nutrients help with the healing process—although whether they reduce acute muscle inflammation is debatable. For example, papaya's high levels of vitamin C and antioxidants eliminate free radicals that damage cells while possibly promoting bone growth and repairing connective tissue. Most sources of protein like eggs aid recovery. Other protein options include nuts and seeds with vitamin E (another antioxidant) to form new tissue; whey protein, which prevents muscle breakdown and builds new tissue; and salmon, which seems to alleviate some muscle soreness by serving as a natural aspirin. Vitamin A foods, such as spinach, may also aid tissue repair.

As you can see, dancers need to aim for specific nutritional goals to perform at their peak, avoid injuries, and heal. Obviously, these goals are easier to achieve if you can cook, rather than relying on take-out foods, delicatessens, and restaurants.

Food Preparation

Ellen Sorrin, director of the George Balanchine Trust, which licenses his ballets to companies and schools worldwide, is an admitted food lover. Every year she teaches NYCB dancers how to prepare healthy, nutritious, and easy recipes that support their busy lifestyle; her lessons are supplemented with informative handouts. Additionally, dancers who want a simple primer on preparing healthy, convenient options can attend a basic class with our nutritionist. Luckily, following recipes is not a challenge for the dancers. Sorrin says, "Dancers get things done. They know how to follow directions because it's what they do in the ballet studio every day." In fact, after our dancers had their first class with her, they were eager to learn more.

Overall, young dancers straight out of training appear to need the most help learning to prepare food, especially the young men. However, I know for a fact that some female dancers also feel lost when it comes to food preparation because I was one of them. Learning the basics can really help you meet your nutritional goals. For example, an easy approach to healthy eating is to mix and match. Breakfast could be a fruit smoothie with 1 percent milk or a whole-grain cereal with a handful of berries and sliced bananas. Apples, pears, or melons make a healthy addition to lunch. Besides being a great source of energy, fruit's natural sweetness makes it a delicious snack. Look for ways to add fruits to your food plan throughout the day. Just watch out for the added sugar in yogurt and canned or frozen products. Instead, buy plain low-fat yogurt and mix in your favorite fresh or dried fruit. The same goes for cottage cheese.

If you want to roast vegetables, think global! Add them to Italian whole-wheat pasta, pile them on top of a piece of French fish like sole, or put them in a Mexican tortilla or a New York deli wrap. The same philosophy applies to cooking chicken, which can last in the refrigerator for three to four days. In addition to being part of a hot dinner, chicken can be added to a tasty sandwich with lettuce and Dijon mustard or on top of a Caesar salad as a great protein source. If you are feeling adventurous, you can mix roasted vegetables and chicken together with some eggs and a dash of parmesan cheese to make a flat Italian omelet or frittata. Stews, sides, salsas, and pasta sauces are also open to experimentation. As always, fresh is best, but you do not have to eat vegetables raw. While some fruits and vegetables with complex vitamins like C and B lose nutrients with cooking, cancer-fighting lycopene, found in tomatoes and other red fruits, needs heat to be released. Heating foods to 188 degrees Fahrenheit makes protein and fiber easier to digest.

Frozen and canned vegetables are also fine as long as they are low in sodium. (Hint: Draining the liquid from the can reduces the amount of added salt.) Because excess sodium is often added to cheese spreads, a better solution is to eat natural low-fat cheese. The government recommends 2,400 mg of sodium a day. Dancers may want to stay closer to 2,000 mg—less than a single teaspoon of salt—to keep from bloating while replenishing what is lost through sweat. You can control excess fat and salt intake by limiting salad dressings, sodium-filled breads like hamburger buns, butter, and salt from the salt shaker. Feel free to add spices such as dill, oregano, basil, or parsley for extra flavor. You can also log on to the Web site for the supermarket chain Hannaford Brothers, which has developed a nutritional index called Guiding Stars that rates grocery foods by the quantity of vitamins, minerals, dietary fiber, and whole grains in each item (at www .hannaford.com). Points are taken away for trans fat, saturated fat, and added salt and sugar, so you can make educated decisions about what to purchase. Some snacks that received top ratings include grapes, plain yogurt with additions like sliced almonds or fresh fruit, whole-wheat pita bread with hummus and vegetables, and popcorn. While there is a place for no-star foods in every balanced diet, it never hurts to aim for the best.

Common Obstacles to Healthy Eating

Obviously, motivation is the key to learning to cook, planning menus, and trying new foods. Yet it still isn't easy to eat the right foods. Lack of appetite, emotional eating, and time constraints may stand in your way from time to time. Here's how to deal with these issues.

LACK OF APPETITE. Exercise, combined with inconsistent eating, can wreak havoc with your appetite. Should you eat if you're not hungry? Yes, just be aware that intense exercise can put a damper on your appetite right afterward. Lucy, a modern dancer, often has to force herself to eat because she has almost no appetite after dancing. To make it easier, she now eats five or six small meals each day instead of three larger meals. You can also use meal replacements like Ensure Plus for snacks because the body only registers volume from food, not fluids. Whatever you do, please do not save your biggest meal for nighttime. Jerry, who is in a contemporary dance company, knows from personal experience how this can backfire. Because he would always eat a large meal after the show, he was never hungry in the morning—a nasty feeling. While it sounds a bit like a cliché, breakfast is still the most important meal of the day, especially for dancers, whose bodies can only store a limited amount of carbohydrates for energy.

EMOTIONAL EATING. Whether you are happy or sad, emotions can trigger urges for junk food. What can you do when a craving threatens to overwhelm you? Unlike physical hunger, which builds up gradually, the urge to eat for emotional reasons develops suddenly. Plus, because you aren't eating in response to hunger, you can't stop in response to fullness. The tendency is to make irrational decisions and choose unhealthy foods high in calories, fat, and sugar. Happy feelings can be a cause for celebration so you gorge on relatively healthy junk foods. Would you believe that pizza gets top billing among this group because of the calcium and protein in cheese and the vitamins in dough and tomato sauce (as well as cancer-fighting lycopene)? Similar urges to reach for junk food occur when you're down in the dumps—only this time the craving often tends to be for carbohydrates and fat for women (desserts) and protein and fat for men (burgers). NYCB corps member Elizabeth Walker knows too well how food can be an emotional crutch. She counters this by using a variety of stress-management tools, including writing in a journal. Elizabeth also eats foods high in fiber, like apples and nuts, to stabilize her blood sugar.

TIME CONSTRAINTS. Most of you high achievers juggle many re-sponsibilities. How do you eat responsibly if you have homework, auditions, or back-to-back rehearsals? There are ways to get around these obstacles. For example, time constraints affect all busy dancers. Janie, who is auditioning for Broadway shows, learned that grocery shopping at the beginning of the week is a great time saver because it allows her to pack healthy snacks like trail mix in her dance bag. She also has food for breakfast, lunch, and dinner at her fingertips. Still, it can be difficult for some dancers to shop for kitchen supplies without a list of must-have items. Those of you who would like help setting up a bare-bones kitchen can check out Appendix G. (And to see how the size of your dishes affects how much you eat, check out Chapter 8.) You'll find simple lists of useful kitchen utensils like pots and pans, basic food staples for the pantry and refrigerator, and handy recipe books. Even Diana, who considers herself cuisine-challenged, wasn't intimidated. Dance students who are stuck with cafeteria food should steer clear of anything fried, while zeroing in on healthy choices, such as the salad bar, white poultry meat, veggie burgers, peanut butter and jelly sandwiches on whole-grain bread, fruit, plain yogurt, and low-fat milk or cottage cheese.

Now that you know about the obstacles as well as the road to healthy eating, you're ready to examine different dancers' eating habits over a twenty-four-hour period.

A Day in the Life of Three Dancers

Because your stomach registers food volume (not calories), it is easy to over- or undereat without even noticing it. This is especially true for beverages. The final step for those of you who want to change your eating habits is to keep track of what you eat to see if it is suf-ficient for dancing, in addition to dealing with your appetite, emo-tions, and time constraints. Check out the following scenarios to see if you can spot common red flags to unhealthy eating. You will then learn the nuts and bolts of keeping a food diary.

The Conscientious Dancer

Susan is a typical sixteen-year-old dancer who has decided to become an ovo-vegetarian because she adores animals. She refuses to eat any animal products other than eggs—no milk or milk products—because of her beliefs. It's only been nine months, but she feels healthy and good about herself. Here is a day in her life.

It's eight o'clock in the morning. Susan notes anxious feelings about the day because one spot on the top of her foot hurts. It has been like that for three weeks. Her periods have stopped for the last six months, but she assumes this is temporary. Still, she makes sure to eat her standard breakfast, even though her stomach is a bit queasy because of her nerves. Breakfast includes a big cup of herbal tea with honey, a handful of granola cereal mixed in with a small, 1-ounce box of raisins, and two cups of spring water. She places snacks, a new pair of pointe shoes, and a BPA-free plastic water bottle in her dance bag and takes off for her first ballet class of the day. (While the jury is out about the potential dangers of bisphenol A, identified by the recycling number 7 on certain plastic goods, go to www.ewg.org/node/20944 for more information.)

During technique class, Susan is relieved that her foot feels okay—at least until the end, when she begins to jump. She ices it afterward like a good dancer, and the pain goes away. So far, so good. Susan also remembers to take several large sips from her water bottle when she's thirsty. She then spends the next two hours sewing ribbons on her toe shoes and doing her homework.

Realizing that she forgot to eat the roasted soybeans that she packed with a hard-boiled egg for snacks, Susan adds the soybeans to her 1:30 P.M. lunch: a mixed green salad with 2 ounces of tofu and three tablespoons of diet Italian dressing. She drinks two cups of herbal tea with honey and feels proud of avoiding the bagels in the cafeteria (her secret vice). Her mind is on the next class, where she will get to dance variations from *Sleeping Beauty*. Ignoring the achy feelings in her foot, she warms up, bangs on her new pointe shoes to soften them, and fills the box with lambswool to cushion her toes so no one suspects that her foot is killing her or that she is feeling pooped. In fact, her teacher compliments her on the height of her last grand jeté.

It's four thirty in the afternoon. Susan feels a bit dizzy, sore, and upset. What if she cannot dance as well tomorrow? She wolfs down a small bag of jelly beans, instead of her hard-boiled egg, and heads for home. Dinner is a soy burger with lots of vegetables and 16 ounces of water. She is exhausted and falls asleep at quarter to nine in the evening during her favorite television show, *American Idol*.

What Are Susan's Red Flags? In looking over her day, we see several problems. First, while Susan wants to be healthy, her total food intake seems insufficient for dance. If she were to count up her calories and fat grams, Susan would find that she's eating far less than she needs during the day. Next, the desire to be an ovo-vegetarian, while understandable for ethical reasons, makes it difficult for her to get enough protein, calcium, and other nutrients to meet the needs of a growing girl, let alone a dancer. This is probably why her menses have stopped. Meanwhile, her sore foot could be a stress reaction; only an orthopedist can tell. Her lack of menses may be contributing to the problem.

It's easy to see from Susan's behavior that her mood affects her eating: for example, heading for the jelly beans after her foot starts to hurt. However, part of her craving for candy may also be due to low blood sugar, since she's forgetting to eat her snacks while doing her homework. Lack of hydration is an equal concern. Susan isn't drinking enough water throughout class or rehydrating afterward. She drinks only when she is thirsty and feels dizzy and fatigued. She is not taking a multivitamin or calcium supplements with vitamin D.

The Remedy Susan's mom needs to schedule a complete physical checkup for her daughter with an internist, an endocrinologist, and an orthopedist. Susan also needs to work with a registered dietician to ensure that she meets all of her needs as an ovo-vegetarian since she is not menstruating. A diet dressing, with its added sugar and salt, is not the best way to meet her need for healthy fats. On the positive side, she is young and probably has not done permanent damage to her body yet. She needs to use the food diary to keep track of her intake throughout the day (in spite of homework assignments), while adding essential calories, vitamins, and minerals.

The Broadway Gypsy

Michael is a theater dancer who moves from show to show while making the rounds of auditions. His way of dealing with another day's fruitless search for work is to order a giant cheeseburger with a side order of fried onion rings and play video games. He couldn't care less about grocery shopping, having breakfast, or cooking. However, because he wants to eat better to make it as a performer, Michael decides to be on his best behavior. See what you think.

After going to sleep at two in the morning, Michael manages to wake up for his early jazz class and eat breakfast. Remembering some tips from a nutrition lecture at his former college dance program, he gulps down two cereal bars with a glass of skim milk at nine in the morning, followed by an orange on his long subway ride from his inexpensive Brooklyn apartment to Manhattan. He also drinks 16 ounces of water an hour before dancing. Even after wrenching his back in a jazz combination, he remembers to sip two more cups of water during class. Snacks, while never a strong point, include trail mix to refuel, while continuing to drink water for three hours. Michael is surprised to find that he feels full of energy.

The next stop is lunch, followed by his singing lesson. At this point, his back is stiff, but he keeps to his schedule, ordering a turkey sandwich with lettuce on rye bread and a 20-ounce bottle of lime-flavored "enhanced" water with electrolytes. Michael knows that turkey is healthy, and the label on the front of his drink says it's the perfect way to jump-start the day. What could be better? The weird part is that he feels hungry soon afterward and grabs a blueberry muffin. Later, he is tired, irritable, *and* hungry. He ignores his cravings for sugar and heads out for his acting class. His main concern is whether he can remember his lines.

Acting class is okay, except for a few mistakes. Michael drinks a beer, orders in a sushi deluxe with assorted raw fish, rice, and vegetables (spinach, cucumber, carrots, and seaweed) with low-sodium soy sauce, followed by two more glasses of water. He nurses his sore back with a warm bath. While Michael knows today's food intake was better than usual, somehow he expected more and feels bummed out.

What Are Michael's Red Flags? You might think that his desire for take-out food is the problem. However, Michael has done an excellent job in choosing healthy meals with sufficient calories, while staying well hydrated. If anything, his only mistakes include being sleep-deprived and believing the hoopla on food packaging, specifically the part about "enhanced" drinks.

Let's begin with the sleep factor. In general, tired dancers do not clear sugars from their bodies as efficiently as their well-rested colleagues. Sleep deprivation also triggers hunger pangs and carbohydrate cravings, while causing the body to burn calories more slowly. Michael isn't overweight yet. However, the muffin craving (refined grains) and his increasing hunger suggest that he needs more sleep. His lime-flavored water probably contributed to his declining mood and energy. It has 25 grams of sugar (more than a Hershey chocolate bar), which he would have seen if he had bothered to check the label on the back. No wonder he was worried about his ability to concentrate during his acting class. Finally, while his overall food choices are good, drinking alcohol (beer) can increase swelling in any injury.

The Remedy Michael got his act together fast. All he needs to do is get more sleep, stay away from enhanced drinks and beer (when injured), and have more water. My only other concern is that he may not be getting in quite enough food. He could calculate his approximate food intake with a calorie counter available at www.thecaloriecounter .com). And a food diary would also help. He could use a multivitamin with minerals and stop being so hard on himself. After all, he did a good job.

The Touring Contemporary Dancer

Judy has achieved her dream—to perform in a major contemporary dance company. The downside is that they tour constantly, although she enjoys seeing Europe and Asia. It has also been an incredible adventure to learn about other cultures. Her only pet peeve is her growing waistline. Judy is worried that eating out at restaurants is making her fat. She decides to keep tabs on her food intake to see if she's on the right track.

It's 8:15 A.M. when Judy waltzes over to the buffet table in the restaurant at her hotel in Beijing. After looking over the traditional Chinese breakfast of fried bread, scallion pancakes, rice gruel, and "thousand-year-old" eggs, she decides to pass. Instead, she goes for more familiar food, loading up her plate with scrambled eggs, sausages, several slices of buttered white toast, and two glasses of orange juice. Because she believes in eating everything on her plate, she gobbles it all up, drinks a cup of light coffee, and heads for company class.

Armed with a couple of protein bars (brought from home) and her trusty water bottle, she changes into her dance clothes. She drinks approximately 16 ounces of water before settling into her thirty-minute warmup. Class starts soon after and she continues to sip water as her body is bathed in sweat. For some reason, she feels a bit sluggish. Later, she munches on a protein bar and drinks more water. She's looking forward to getting out with her friends for lunch. At noon, they all meet at a local place for brown rice, vegetables, and chicken with tea. Judy thinks how much easier it would be in the United States to stop off at McDonald's, but she knows that a large order of fries won't cut it if she wants to be lean. Oh, well.

It's time to rehearse for a few hours before heading back to the hotel. She nibbles on another boring protein bar during an afternoon break at three o'clock, drinks her water, and runs through the dance piece for that night's performance. At least she has roasted duck with orange sauce waiting for her after the show (her favorite!), rice, of course, and vegetables. She might have some wine with dinner. The calorie counting isn't working with restaurant food. She'll just wing it.

What Are Judy's Red Flags? It is not her inability to count calories. In fact, it's quite difficult to calculate how many calories you are consuming unless the restaurant lists the calories on its menu or you get the information online (www.thecaloriecounter.com). Judy is also in a foreign country, adding to the confusion. However, her frustration in dealing with these issues has led her to chuck the whole idea of keeping an eye on her food intake. Too bad—it might have helped her manage her choices better as well as work on portion control.

For example, regardless of what country you are visiting, you can notice whether you're loading up your plate (especially at a buffet) and eating every last bit. It is also easy to consider your food choices. In Judy's case, she tended to veer toward foods high in fat (sausages and duck), sugar (juice), and that yummy orange sauce at dinner. Yet there are also signs of healthy eating in her choices, including eggs, produce, brown rice, and chicken. Still, if she went over her food choices in her mind at the end of the day, she would have seen that she felt "sluggish" before class—a sign that she ate too much.

Judy's snacks and water were fine. However, the lack of variety is getting to her. She feels bored with the protein bars. After a while, this could lead her to skip them altogether. Lunch was okay if not especially exciting. This may have made her overly receptive to a tasty dinner, which turned out to be another high-calorie extravaganza.

The Remedy The first rule of thumb when filling your plate is to take only 80 percent of what you think you will need and leave something on the plate after you finish. A buffet can be extremely tempting, because we are hardwired to go for variety. As a result, Judy would be better off getting eggs and filling the rest of her plate with fresh fruit, and having a spicy lunch. The easiest way to handle restaurant food is to split portions or eat two appetizers instead of an entrée. Ask for sauce on the side. A cup of roasted duck can add up to 600 calories (not counting the sauce) and 50 grams of fat.

Keeping a Food Diary

Obviously, it helps to know what you are eating, as well as the triggers. A food diary records three or four important pieces of information regarding your daily food intake: the time you eat and drink, what you consume, how you feel, and the amount of calories and fat (optional). Diana, our young dancer introduced at the beginning of this chapter, has been keeping her diary while working with her registered dietician. Let's see how she does after four weeks of nutritional counseling. Her food diary is recorded in the accompanying table. (If you would like to keep a food diary, a blank worksheet is provided in Appendix H.)

As her food record shows, Diana stayed within her caloric range for an active female dancer who took one to two daily technique classes.

Diana's Daily Food Diary

TIME	FOOD/LIQUIDS	FEELINGS	CALORIES/ FAT (GRAMS)
Breakfast 7:45 A.M.	1 cup hot oatmeal w/ 6 oz. blueberries, 1 cup 1% milk	Woke up early for breakfast. Excited about dance class.	282/6
8:30 A.M.	3 cups cold water (1 cup 30 min. prior to class, 2 cups during class)	Worried about bloating.	
Snack 10:50 A.M.	1 oz. part-skim mozzarella cheese, 1 cup Gatorade	Great class! Lots of energy, plus no bloating! Wow!	138/5
Lunch 1:00 P.M.	1 turkey sandwich on whole wheat w/ butterhead leaves and mustard, 1 orange, coffee w/ 1% milk	Feel content, not hungry, and happy w/ food choices, so hope I can keep it up.	460/17
1:30 P.M.	3 cups cold water (1 cup 30 min. prior to class, 2 cups during class)	Felt light in adagio class.	
Snack 4:00 P.M.	1 plain yogurt, ½ cup raisins, 2 cups cold water	Often eat candy at this time. Can't believe I'm not tempted.	372/5
Dinner 8:00 P.M.	1 lean pork chop, w/ 8 oz. green beans, 1 glass white wine, 1 sm. chocolate chip cookie	Didn't expect the adagio class to go so well, but had a big argument with my roommate over nothing.	414/11
Snack 8:45 P.M.	2 cups mint tea w/ honey, 2 oz. roasted peanuts	Upset about fight and eating nuts. Feel full.	452/18
		Total:	2118/62

Diana ate a nice balance of carbohydrates and lean protein, stayed sufficiently hydrated, and paced her food throughout the day. She didn't let her concern about becoming bloated stop her from drinking water, even though it was right before being partnered in adagio class. Diana also had only one small chocolate chip cookie versus her usual bag of jelly beans. The only area where her mood seems to have had an effect is when she ate peanuts after arguing with her roommate, bringing her total fat intake to 62 grams. This is still close to a normal range for dancers (40 to 60 grams). My only advice is, keep up the good work!

The Bottom Line

A balanced diet for dancers involves a variety of nutritious foods. This can be challenging for several reasons, including lack of appetite from exercise, emotional eating, and time constraints—in addition to having to prepare your own food. Yet the rewards are tangible and will have a direct and positive impact on your dancing. When all is said and done, dancers need to be food-conscious, not food-phobic! Think about what you're getting in, not what you're avoiding. It's a much healthier way to look at it.

EIGHT

Effective Weight
Control Strategies

I struggled with my weight for years. Now, I know a moderate approach
to the way I eat and use the gym works best.

—JENIFER RINGER, NYCB principal

Weight control is an issue for many dancers who judge themselves on their appearance. However, the desire to be fit and lean doesn't have to trigger disordered eating, which threatens not only your dancing but your physical and mental well-being. Dieting is a trap filled with false promises. Don't be fooled. There are healthy ways to reach and maintain an optimal weight by working with, rather than against, your body. This chapter will show you how to do it, using the latest scientific principles in weight management to help you achieve your goals.

Every dancer's body is different, but then so are the aesthetic requirements in the various branches of dance. Some techniques, like ballet, call for a leaner look, whereas others are less focused on a particular silhouette. For example, a "normal" body often is considered the ideal in many modern dance companies. Even Broadway and commercial dance showcase curvier women and sturdier men onstage. Artistic directors also may prefer physiques that aren't rail-thin, while others make allowances for special talent. Dance is a more diverse arena than most aspiring professionals realize. Still, no one is immune from society's mantra to be thin or the dangers of dieting, least of all dancers.

LEFT (Jenifer Ringer and Benjamin Millepied in Jerome Robbins's *Dances at a Gathering*)

Jenifer's Story

NYCB ballerina Jenifer Ringer learned about the serious repercussions of dieting the hard way. The biggest deception is that the first diet can seem easy. Reduce your food intake to the bare minimum of calories and the weight disappears. Simple! That is, until your body's survival mechanism kicks into high gear, setting you up to binge. A small proportion of dancers withstand the urge to eat and become anorexic (a potentially fatal illness). Most, like Jenifer, cycle through periods of dieting and overeating—and ultimately, weight gain. As a result, Jenifer wasn't cast in her old roles and her emotional state deteriorated. Jenifer recalls, "I hated the fact that I was so heavy. I wasn't able to dance, which is what brought me so much joy, and when I did get onstage I hated it. It felt like everyone was just looking at how horrible I was."

Jenifer set out on her diet with the best intentions without knowing how the body reacts to caloric restriction. This fact was her undoing. You'll find out how her story ends later in this chapter. Needless to say, the way that you go about changing your weight is key to a successful outcome.

The Ups and Downs of Dieting

Many images come to mind when you think of dieting. I doubt most of them are positive. "Diet," which comes from the Latin word *diaeta* meaning "a way of living," requires a long-term commitment. Most weight-loss diets lead to feelings of hunger, deprivation, and failure, as people regain the lost weight and then some. At the other end of the spectrum are food plans aimed at weight gain (especially for young men) that produce a potbelly in lieu of the promised Adonis-like figure. While you may want to maintain or reach a certain weight for a branch of dance that demands a long, lean look, there are real pitfalls.

Dancers need food to learn, improve, rehearse, perform, succeed, and avoid injuries. Still, a large survey by *Dance Magazine,* described in my book *Advice for Dancers,* indicates that one out of two dancers struggle with disordered eating and 4 percent meet all of the clinical criteria for eating disorders. Early warning signs may indicate a subclinical problem, requiring further evaluation. For eating disorder specialists and services, contact the Renfrew Center at www .renfrewcenter.com.

Anorexia nervosa is a deadly disease that often begins during the early teen years, endangering health and career by diminishing bone density, causing muscle wasting (including the heart), and affecting virtually every organ in the body. It pays to be aware of the early warning signs; if the signs are ignored, serious consequences may result.

Early Warning Signs of Anorexia Nervosa

- Concerned about eating in public
- Skips meals with family or friends
- Uses caffeine or gum in place of food
- Exercises more than normal
- Preoccupied with weight, shape, and calories
- Looks gaunt and weak while dancing

Sarah, a talented sixteen-year-old ballet student, decided to lose weight after enrolling in a highly renowned dance school. Feeling insecure, she chose to increase her competitive edge by cutting way back on calories and by exercising compulsively. She dropped twenty pounds in six months—much to the horror of her school director, who (thankfully) refused to let her dance and asked her mother to take her for a medical evaluation. Sarah displayed all of the criteria for anorexia nervosa established by the American Psychiatric Association:

- Significant weight loss (or failure to make expected weight gains), more than 15 percent below ideal, based on published weight–height tables

- Intense fear of becoming fat or gaining weight in spite of being underweight

- Disturbed perception of body, self-evaluation overly tied to weight, and denial of health risks (only one of these is required for a diagnosis)

- Amenorrhea (loss of menses for three or more consecutive months or failure to get menses without hormone therapy)

Anorexics may restrict their food intake, overexercise, or binge and purge by vomiting or misusing laxatives, diuretics, or enemas.

Fortunately, Sarah received treatment at the Renfrew Center before her health deteriorated significantly. She also was motivated to regain the lost weight and eat properly in order to dance. (Be aware that these days school and company directors are much more likely to ask you to stop dancing and seek medical help if you lose an excessive amount of weight).

In contrast, dancers who develop bulimia nervosa generally have a later onset (ages fourteen to eighteen) and maintain a body weight at or slightly above or below normal levels. However, this disorder is also fraught with serious health threats, such as stomach problems, dental decay, electrolyte imbalances, an irregular heartbeat, and a ruptured esophagus. Some of these problems had already begun to affect Ella, a seventeen-year-old musical theater student who had planned to start auditioning until her brother teased her about her curvy figure, calling her Ella the Elephant. She started off by fasting, using diet pills to quell her hunger pangs. However, this approach quickly spun out of control. Ella began to drink to calm her jittery nerves and improve her mood, and would then binge and purge. (Substance abuse occurs in at least 30 percent of bulimics.) This behavior lasted for almost a year. She finally sought medical help after spitting up blood one day. Ella met all of the following criteria established for bulimia nervosa.

- Repeatedly bingeing on excessive amounts of food (for example, a whole pizza and quart of ice cream) within a two-hour period while feeling out of control

- Using inappropriate compensatory behaviors, such as vomiting, misuse of enemas, diuretics, or laxatives; fasting; compulsive exercise to prevent weight gain

- Bingeing and trying to forestall weight gain through unhealthy behaviors at least twice a week for three months

- Basing self-evaluation on body weight and shape to an excessive degree

Like anorexics, some bulimics diet, fast, or exercise compulsively, whereas others purge. Both types of eating disorders are associated with anxiety and depression.

While Ella eventually recovered with treatment and went back to dance, she could have averted a lot of self-loathing, health problems, and lost career opportunities if someone had noticed the early warning signs of this disorder. A similar eating problem, called binge-eating disorder, involves all of the symptoms of bulimia without unhealthy attempts at weight loss.

Early Warning Signs of Bulimia Nervosa

- Dramatic weight fluctuations

- Preoccupation with dieting

- Overindulging in food

- Using bathroom after eating

- Food disappearances

- Chipmunk look and raw knuckles from vomiting

If you fear that you are falling into any of these destructive eating patterns, please seek professional help. The Renfrew Center offers a variety of excellent programs, as well as a Web site for friends and families seeking advice. For an inspirational book that equates recovering from an eating disorder with leaving an abusive relationship, check out *Life Without Ed*. Further resources about eating disorders are listed in Appendix A.

Finally, dance schools and companies can work with health-care professionals to establish a goal weight for anorexic dancers to return to class or performing. Sharing information requires a signed release, compliant with current privacy health rules. In no case should artistic administrators require any dancer other than anorexics to be weighed, as this tends to create excessive weight concerns and eating problems.

Navigating the Road to Weight Change

As you see from the above scenarios, rapid weight loss can jeopardize your health and well-being. Whether you like it or not, years of evolution have programmed your body to equate calorie restriction with starvation. Enter the genetic set point, which keeps you hovering around that same old number on the scale. Go on an 800-calorie diet and your metabolism will slow down by almost half, thereby conserving calories. Efforts to increase your natural weight are equally accompanied with obstacles, because a large percentage of body mass, no matter where you are on the continuum from thin to obese, is predetermined by your genes. This predisposition appears to kick in at birth. Rapid weight gain during the first week of life is associated with weight problems three decades later! One healthy way to burn calories is through slow, long-distance aerobic exercise for forty to sixty minutes at 65 percent MHR, four times per week.

In addition to one's set point, gender differences add to the dieter's quandary. On average, men have a faster basal metabolic rate (BMR) than women because of greater amounts of lean muscle mass. BMR is the amount of calories that you burn at rest. BMR accounts for 70 percent of the body's total daily energy output needed to support such vital functions as heartbeat, breathing, and core temperature. Other calorie burners include activity level and digestion, with the latter expending approximately 10 percent of your daily food intake.

To see how this works, compare two twenty-year-old dancers,

one male and one female, who are both five-foot-five and weigh the same amount (the ideal weight for height and gender). According to the Harris-Benedict BMR equation (www.gymgoal.com/dtool_bmr .html), the male dancer is burning 211 more calories a day than his female counterpart (1,620 versus 1,409 calories, respectively). This discrepancy amounts to a whopping 6,330 calories a month.

Still, it's difficult for many people to conform to the ideal body in different dance forms, no matter the gender. NYCB dietician Joy Bauer says, "A lot of times we're fighting women's genes and appetite to help them be thin. At the same time, most of the young men are burning a gazillion calories when what they need is to build muscle to lift the dancers." Both groups benefit from education in nutrition, says Bauer. Equally important is getting a clean bill of health from your doctor. An under- or overactive thyroid, along with medications (for example, some antidepressants), can have a significant impact on metabolism. But current birth control pills no longer present a weight-control problem, according to endocrinologist Dr. Michelle Warren.

Dieting Pitfalls

Changing your natural set point for weight is filled with pitfalls, whether you want to go up or down. Men would seem to face less hassle than women, yet those who need to build muscle are often just as confused as dancers who have to lose weight. For example, in going above your set point, the tendency is to eat everything under the sun for rapid weight gain. Even if you eat healthy foods, gaining over a pound a week adds more fat than muscle. The exception is recovering from anorexia nervosa; then you need excess calories just to acquire normal levels of body fat and muscle, especially as your metabolism speeds up with nutritious eating. It's a misconception to think that recovering anorexics have permanently altered their metabolism, says Dr. Warren.

Typically, rapidly moving above your set point causes you to lose your appetite as the body tries to regulate your weight. It takes roughly 3,500 extra calories over the course of a week for young men to gain a pound. This is difficult to sustain, especially if you feel stuffed. Often the result is skipped meals, which has the effect of slowing your metabolic rate so you gain more fat. Excess protein beyond the 20 percent allotted for healthy dancing is unnecessary. However, you will need to combine weight training (see page 83) with your food intake to increase the size of your muscles.

Not surprisingly, even more problems await those who try to lose weight too quickly. If you drop more than two pounds a week, your body will fight you. The first backlash may be intense food cravings, and this will set you up for binge eating. If you lose 10 percent of your body weight, you will burn 23 percent fewer calories per day, making it harder to lose weight and easier to gain it back. In fact, dieting often leads to weight gain, according to Dr. Dianne Neumark-Sztainer, who studies eating behaviors in teenagers at the University of Minnesota School of Public Health. Rapid weight loss may result not only in lost fat, but also lost bone density and muscle—not a good strategy for achieving peak performance or preventing injury.

Dangers of Crash Diets

- Insufficient nutrients
- Breakdown of muscles
- Weakness and fatigue
- Decreased metabolic rate
- Increased hunger

Popular diets that peel off the pounds quickly cause the body to go into starvation mode. Many of these diets work by reducing your daily caloric intake. With too few calories coming in, your body must find another source of energy. It does so by burning body fat and lean muscle. Ridding yourself of excess fat may sound good, but the problem is that it causes the body to secrete less of the hormone leptin, which helps you regulate menstruation and make new bones.

Endocrinologist Dr. Michelle Warren has found that young dancers who restrict their diets by consuming insufficient calories and protein have a higher rate of stress fractures, owing to a significant delay in puberty (onset of menses at sixteen or older). This is a diet-related problem. Meanwhile, no dancer can afford to lose muscle. Besides slowing your metabolic rate, you lose strength and stamina. The clincher is that fighting your body's hunger signals can result in disordered eating, leading to the female athlete triad: eating problems, menstrual irregularity, and brittle bones.

If your body has shut down because of excessive dieting, you need to follow a well-balanced meal plan and maintain a healthy body mass. (BMI is not a useful tool for assessing healthy elite athletes whose extra muscles make them appear fatter than they are. This isn't an issue for dancers.) Frequently, those who diet excessively will have primary amenorrhea (delayed menses) or secondary amenorrhea (no menses for three or more months). Contrary to past belief, hormone replacement therapy will not protect bone density in young women. Menstruation is an indirect sign that your body has enough fat to function normally, so it's best not to mask the problem by taking hormones. Until menses happen naturally, Dr. Warren recommends an annual bone scan of the hip and spine to monitor the state of your bones.

Body Mass Index

<18.5	Too thin
18.5–24.9	Healthy
25.0–29.9	Overweight
>30.0	Obese

To calculate BMI, go to www.bariatricedge.com and enter your age, sex, weight, and height.

Older dancers who have a history of amenorrhea need to get a bone scan at age fifty because of a heightened risk of osteoporosis at menopause, says Dr. Warren. Men are also subject to osteoporosis, albeit at a lower rate than women. You should discuss various treatment options for bone loss, including medications, with your doctor.

Weight Gain

Assuming that you want to gain lean muscle (which many male and some female dancers do), you will need to eat just over what your body requires to maintain its natural weight, combined with special weight training. A three-day food diary will give you an idea of your current intake. This is your baseline. The next step is to increase this amount by 300 calories, or what food researcher Dr. Brian Wansink refers to as the "mindless margin." Besides avoiding any discomfort from rapidly moving beyond your set point, you eliminate excess food that could be stored as fat. There is no need to increase your protein intake beyond 15 to 20 percent of total daily food intake. The goal is to gain no more than half a pound per week. The only exception to this approach is in the case of anorexia nervosa, where you would add up to 500 calories to your daily intake each week, according to registered dietician Laura Pumillo.

Once your weight plateaus, add another 300 calories to your weekly food intake until your body adjusts. Meanwhile, it's important to follow a healthy food schedule by eating every three to four hours. Begin with breakfast to jump-start your metabolism, which has slowed down during sleep. NYCB principal Joaquin De Luz, who lost fat while gaining muscle, is a firm believer in "starting the day with a super breakfast like several egg whites with toast and some meat." He also eats every few hours to keep his metabolism up. "I feel great, with plenty of energy," says Joaquin. (While muscle size is determined by your genes, you can reach your body's full potential with a sensible food plan, plus heavy weights and sprinting three times a week for twenty-minute sessions during easy work schedules.)

Weight Loss

The same approach applies to weight loss: Slowly decrease your calories, cutting no more than 300 calories a week from your current daily intake (use a three-day food diary to determine your baseline). Never go below your basal metabolic rate, the rate at which your body burns calories to keep vital organs functioning. You can calculate your BMR using your age, gender, height, and weight at www.gymgoal.com/dtool_bmr.html. It's also important to do slow, long-distance aerobics three to four times a week for forty to sixty minutes to lower your set point and burn calories. Choose a routine that does not build bulky muscles, such as the elliptical machine or moderate exercise on the stationary bike, and add a conditioning program like yoga, Pilates, or Gyrotonic to increase lean body mass. Again, the goal is to lose weight slowly to avoid hunger or triggering the body to go into conservation mode. Aim for one-half to two pounds a week.

Abi Stafford explains how she achieves these goals: "I eat a large breakfast and snack whenever I'm hungry. I try to eat another substantial meal before the show and replenish my body afterward." In addition to eating small, nutritious snacks throughout the day, she uses a moderate setting on the stationary bike (under 10 mph) to lower her genetic set point for weight without bulking up. Abi also does Pilates three times per week to increase lean muscle mass during rehearsal periods.

A dieting question that often comes up for dancers is, "Can I spot-reduce?" Sadly, the answer is no. There is no way to lose weight from a specific part of your body. Be wary of heavily advertised devices that promise great abs but may actually overdevelop other muscle groups. Health-food supplements will also be of no help for weight loss. In addition, because supplements are not FDA-approved, they may contain contaminants. The good news is that by lowering your overall weight (especially with aerobic exercise), you will inadvertently reduce the areas that bother you. This is particularly true for fat on your stomach, which is more easily mobilized than the fat on your hips and thighs. Finally, dancers should know that they will begin to lose muscle mass and gain fat after the age of thirty, making a regular cross-training regimen essential along with changes in eating. Reducing caloric intake by 50 to 100 calories a day for life helps prevent gradual weight gain with age.

Tip

A pound of muscle uses nine times the calories of a pound of fat, helping you stay in shape.

Still, to achieve lasting results in a world where 95 percent of all people who diet fail, you also need to be aware of the impact of sleep deprivation and environmental cues that influence what you eat. This is the last piece of the weight management puzzle.

Lifestyle Factors That Influence Food Intake

Apart from the physiological pitfalls associated with dieting, your lifestyle plays a key role in what you choose to eat. For example, insufficient sleep affects hormones that govern appetite and feelings of satiety. A sixteen-year study by researchers at Case Western University found that women who slept five or fewer hours a night were 32 percent more likely to become overweight by at least thirty pounds than those who got seven or more hours of shut-eye. Ten hours of sleep is ideal for extremely active dancers. If this is impossible to fit into your schedule, aim for a minimum of eight hours per night.

Your environment and eating habits can affect your entire relationship with food, according to psychologist Dr. Brian Wansink, author of *Mindless Eating: Why We Eat More Than We Think*. His research shows that people make over two hundred food decisions a day. Yet few pause to think about what they are doing or stop after every bite to consider if they are full. Instead, they "mindlessly" look for outside signs that say they have eaten enough. One example is finishing everything on your plate. Another is dishing out larger amounts of food from big containers. These visual cues override hunger and taste signals (and judgment).

The size of your plate, bowl, and glass influence the amount of food you eat—by as much as 72 percent. If you want to maintain weight loss (or weight gain), change your dishware, the way you store food, your personal eating habits, and how you eat at restaurants. People are visually oriented when it comes to food. Fool your eyes and you will fool your stomach.

Choose Your Dishware Carefully

Turn your kitchen into a place that doesn't encourage extra food. As you have probably guessed and experienced yourself, the larger the plate, the more you will eat. This is fine if you want to gain weight. Just use 12-inch plates. A regular portion will look puny, so you will be likely to add more food. The same principle applies to large bowls for soups and salads, with larger cutlery. Similarly, you will tend to pour 30 percent more of your beverage into a short, wide drinking glass than into a tall, thin glass, even though the capacity is the same. Use the opposite approach to lose weight. For example, a normal portion on an 8-inch plate looks big. You can also reap rewards by replacing your large, wide wineglasses with smaller ones, the kind generally intended for white wine. Just to be safe, it is easier to give away or store dishware that does not conform to your weight goals than to have to constantly remind yourself.

To prove the point that your eyes can fool you, Dr. Wansink's research shows that moviegoers who were given stale popcorn for free in different-size containers ate 53 percent more from large buckets than from medium-size buckets, simply because they ate what was in front of them. It helps to place all your food on a plate at once so you can see exactly how much you are eating. You are likely to eat 14 percent less food in this way if you take a smaller portion and then consider going back for a second or third helping.

Store Food Appropriately

The main point here is to repackage food into smaller portions, using Tupperware containers or Ziploc bags. Buying food in large quantities is cost-effective, but jumbo boxes will tempt you to eat 25 percent more calories. Other tricks for food storage include wrapping tasty leftovers in aluminum foil and putting them in the back of the refrigerator or freezer so they are out of sight until your next meal. This makes it easier to eat according to your needs, rather than to mindlessly snack on whatever you see when you open the fridge.

Remember Dr. Wansink's "mindless margin," where you eat 300 calories more or less without even noticing it? If you are trying to lose weight, you can take advantage of this by dishing out 20 percent less pasta and adding 20 percent more fruits and vegetables. You can also add a broth-based soup, or put extra greens on a smaller hamburger, or increase air in a fruit smoothie with extra time in the blender. Typically, we tend to serve ourselves the same volume of food for every meal, except on those occasions when we go out to eat. You can make a conscious decision on how you want to balance the food groups. We are always looking for external cues to keep track of how much we eat. These range from weighing ourselves on the scale, to looking in the mirror, to suddenly having trouble fitting into our favorite jeans. This is where weekly weigh-ins plus a food diary come in handy.

Adjust Your Eating Habits

Take control of when and where you eat. While zoning out in front of the television may be relaxing, this tends to make us eat snacks mindlessly. Instead, try eating at the kitchen table without any distractions so that you can become much more mindful of what you put into your mouth. It helps to leave serving dishes of the "good stuff," like potatoes, rice, meat, gravies, and sauces, in the kitchen at least six feet away, while placing salad and vegetables in the middle of the table.

Grocery shopping can be another potential trap and a place in which we tend to go overboard. It is helpful to eat before you go shopping (because hunger tends to make us buy more junk foods), make a grocery list, and focus on the fresh food section. Although the ideal is to be able to eat everything in moderation, certain foods, such as ice cream, may trigger you to overeat. If this is the case, it is safer either to bring one serving home or to replace it entirely with something equally yummy but less caloric, such as strawberries and Cool Whip. Finally, while exercise is a key component of weight control, be aware that you may feel you deserve to eat more because you have been exercising.

Prepare to Eat Out

Going to a nice restaurant can be one of life's pleasures, but splurging at a great place with a beautiful ambiance will likely make you stay longer. Chances are, you will order more food, especially if you are distracted by conversing with others. Eat out with one person and you will consume about 35 percent more calories than usual. Go out with four and you will eat about 75 percent more calories.

In order to combat overeating, eat a snack before dinner so you are not ravenous. Dr. Wansink's research shows that it also helps to model yourself after the slowest eater at the table, because we tend to pace our food intake to match other people. Also, put your eating utensils down while talking so you aren't distracted. Finally, his research indicates that overeaters tend to eat less in front of others, whereas normally light eaters overdo it with company.

To Avoid Overeating in Restaurants

- Stay away from the bread basket.
- Order two out of three: drink, appetizer, dessert.
- Ask for a doggy bag for half of your entrée or order two appetizers.
- Share dessert.

Of course, if you are heading for a buffet a different strategy is in order. Rather than heaping different foods on the plate (which caters to our predilection for variety), choose moderate portions of your two most desired foods, eat them, and then see if you want to go back for more. Chances are, your first plate will be sufficient to quell your hunger—and you will feel satisfied by eating foods that you like.

A Moderate Approach to Weight Control

Now that you are mentally prepared to really tap into this advice, you can use my recommendations for weight control. As you may have guessed, I believe that a moderate approach works best because it includes all the major food groups and does not trigger your body to go into conservation mode or gain fat instead of muscle mass. The simplest route to weight loss is to cut out alcohol, excess sugar, and excess sodium. You can also add or subtract 300 calories in a day without any discomfort, according to Dr. Wansink's research. It helps to use a food diary to keep track of what you eat, along with weekly weigh-ins before breakfast (same time, same scale). You can safely lose between half a pound and two pounds a week. Aim for no more than half a pound a week for weight gain to avoid adding excess fat.

An equally essential part of any weight management program is to maintain lean muscle mass through weight training. If your weight is not changing within two weeks, you can add longer periods of aerobic exercise (one hour, three or four times a week) to reduce, or you can cut back on the amount of aerobics if you are trying to gain weight.

The following guidelines apply in almost all cases to dancers who want to lose weight. First, never eat less than your basal metabolic rate. Doing so is the quickest way to slow your metabolism, lose muscle, send out hunger signals to overeat, and eventually interrupt your menstrual cycle. Second, do not cut out any food group. The ideal dancer's diet is composed of carbohydrates, protein, and fat. Dancers traditionally avoid protein because they associate it with fat. While certain foods high in fat like steak and cheese are not part of a normal weight-loss plan, no food is off-limits in moderation. There are also many low-fat options available, including lean meat, fish, egg whites, and low-fat dairy products high in calcium. Dancers who ignore this food group are more susceptible to stress fractures.

Yet it is easy to fall into the trap of avoiding certain food groups. For example, NYCB corps dancer Dena Abergel thought that if she cut out the fat in her diet, she wouldn't be fat, "and that was a huge mistake," she says. "I also became a vegetarian, so I was depriving myself of specific food, thinking that I was doing something that would help my weight. It was totally counterproductive for weight loss. What eventually ended up working was adding healthy fat and animal protein to my diet."

Every dancer can also benefit from nutritional counseling. NYCB's wellness program requires mandatory evaluations for all incoming dancers. You can get an appropriate referral by contacting the American Dietetic Association (www.eatright.org).

The End of Jenifer Ringer's Story

When we last heard from Jenifer, she was in a battle with her body. Extreme dieting had triggered a vicious cycle of compulsive overeating, leading to significant weight gain. This hurt her self-esteem and career, and she eventually took a leave of absence, believing that she might never dance again. Fortunately, Jenifer used many of the resources described in Chapter 4 to change her behavior. Her strategies included reaching out and receiving unconditional support from her family and religious congregation; letting go of her perfectionism and tendency to always put on a happy face; moderate eating and exercising at the gym; and allowing herself to have a cookie or gain weight during vacations, knowing that she had time to get back in shape. It is a story with a happy ending. She is back dancing with New York City Ballet at her goal weight. She is also proud to be a healthy role model for other dancers. "A lot of times people in the audience will come up to me and say, 'We're so happy that you don't look like you're starving.' That's what I would like to pass on to the younger generation."

A slow, methodical weight loss (or weight gain) program with all the major food groups gives you time for your body to adjust while you develop good eating habits. Remember, rapid changes in weight are fraught with pitfalls. Meanwhile, eating right and exercising go hand in hand, along with managing the visual cues that influence your food intake. When all is said and done, the slowest route to managing your weight is the most effective. This is the weight control plan I recommend for dancers.

Ten Quick Tips for Managing Your Weight

1. Aim for no more than one-half to two pounds of weight loss per week, or no more than one-half pound of weight gain per week.

2. Start off the day with breakfast and refuel every four hours to curb hunger.

3. Preplate your food so that you get a better visual sense of how much you are eating.

4. Eat at the kitchen table rather than mindlessly snacking in front of the TV or computer.

5. Shop for food at the grocery store when you are full, not hungry.

6. At restaurants order a main course and two out of the following three: drink, appetizer, dessert.

7. Don't talk and eat at the same time when dining out with others.

8. At buffets, choose two of your favorite foods rather than many selections.

9. Get at least eight hours of sleep at night to balance the hormones that regulate appetite.

10. Never eat less than your basal metabolic rate (approximate range: 1,200 to 1,500 calories).

NINE

Stress Management Techniques

Dance, like lots of things, is mind over matter. You need a healthy mind before you can have a healthy body.

—MEGAN LECRONE, NYCB corps

S tress is a normal part of life, particularly for dancers who must deal with the pressures of competition, performances, and in- juries in addition to general life events, such as breaking up with a boyfriend. In small quantities, stress can motivate you to rise to the occasion. However, negative long-term stress can often lead to feelings of anger, fatigue, and burnout. The way in which you handle stress will make a significant difference in your ability to thrive in dance, even under difficult circumstances. This chapter will equip you with the tools used by top athletes, such as relaxation exercises, to manage stress and perform at your peak.

Stress can be good or bad, acute or chronic. High performance expectations and demands bring out different reactions in each dancer. For example, Debbie finds initial dance competitions highly pleasur- able, whereas some of her friends feel like they're one step away from an onstage panic attack. Her stress level increases at the second round because she has to prove herself once again to get to the finals, but this is good short-term stress because she feels productive and motivated to perform even better. In contrast, corps dancer Megan LeCrone's problems in dance, which included injuries, were exacerbated—or even caused—by her inner need to be perfect. Megan has had to learn to manage stress with a variety of techniques. "I used to get so ner- vous," she recalls. "Now I don't let it have a negative effect on my performance. I just focus on dancing."

LEFT (Megan LeCrone and Albert Evans in George Balanchine's *Agon*)

Understanding the Stress Response

To perform at your peak, you need to be able to balance your excitement with control. Dancers who are continually out of balance may experience chronic negative stress, which contributes to a host of problems, such as weight gain, delayed wound healing, poor health (for example, numerous colds), and injuries. The remedy differs for each person. In order to identify and address the early signs of stress, be aware of the following:

PERSONAL VULNERABILITIES: general anxiety, overly high standards, excessive self-criticism, inability to accept mistakes, unhealthy coping mechanisms like substance abuse

PHYSICAL SYMPTOMS: muscle tension (backaches and headaches), disordered eating, sleep problems, extreme fatigue, abdominal pain

PSYCHOLOGICAL SYMPTOMS: poor concentration, irritability, forgetfulness, blanking out, constant worrying, social avoidance

The best solution to combating negative stress is prevention. Address the early warning signs before they become serious problems. It is equally important to deal with the underlying causes of stress, such as maladaptive perfectionism. Under the best of circumstances, managing stress can help you grow, take calculated risks, and reach your full potential. The next sections will help you understand and deal with the stress response. I will conclude with showing you how to keep a stress diary to identify and counteract the triggers.

When Stress Is Likely to Strike

A variety of situations can trigger negative stress. In fact, it can arise from any situation or thought that makes you feel upset, anxious, or angry. Tina, for instance, has always been incredibly nervous before auditions. A twenty-three-year-old Broadway dancer with a solid technique, she has begun to go blank in the middle of combinations and even flub steps she knows well. Yet she's desperate to get a job and places extreme pressure on herself to nail each audition by saying, "I have to get hired for this show or I'm no good." The stakes are too high. Plus, she's setting herself up to feel like a failure because getting hired for a musical often depends on factors outside of her control, such as her height and looks. Perhaps the director prefers tall, buxom dancers rather than short, slightly curvaceous ones like Tina. This has nothing at all to do with talent. Still, she feels like she's letting everyone down, especially her parents back home in Wisconsin who want her to succeed. She can't sleep and stays up most of the night worrying about the next audition.

Meanwhile, Edward has all the creature comforts of being in a good ballet company, where he's just been promoted to soloist and gets to perform featured roles. He jokes around to release the nervous tension before going onstage. No one would guess by his jovial attitude, but the stress of his new position and the need to please the director, the critics, and the audience are getting to him. Never one to share his deep emotions, such as anger, frustration, or doubt, he numbs himself with alcohol and marijuana after the performance. The only obvious signs of his distress during the day are a few missed rehearsals; this doesn't go over well with management. Edward makes up excuses, for example, that he had to go to physical therapy—and gets away with it for now. However, the substance abuse is starting to take over his life, and it's only a question of time before it begins to interfere with his performance.

Our last dancer is Rachel, whose career was on a roll in her modern dance school until she overdid it by working too hard and tore her knee ligament. Stress caused by competing with a roomful of other talented dancers led to her predicament. Now she is looking at extensive surgery, followed by months of rehabilitation. It will take at least a year before she is able to go back to dance. All injuries can bring up negative stress for dancers. She has no outside interests (no time before) and now she is hobbling around on crutches in an especially vulnerable situation. Rachel sleeps twelve to fourteen hours per day, snaps at her friends, and avoids invitations to go out. She is also angry with the dancers at her school who are continuing to improve while she sits on the sidelines. Her eating habits have deteriorated and she has gained fifteen pounds, creating even more stress for herself.

It's understandable that auditions, solo roles, and injuries are sources of stress for these dancers. Yet dancers can also get stressed out just from the daily hassles of being a performer as well as from general life events. What makes some dancers more vulnerable to negative stress than others? While there is no simple answer, several factors play a crucial role in your ability to deal with stress. These include differences in personality, coping skills, and the impact of dance injuries. All these, in turn, are mediated by your ability to seek out and accept social support (which is a great stress buster). One quick way to see how stress is affecting you now is to take a self-test that provides personal feedback at www.lessons4living.com.

Personality

One of the main personality factors associated with being gifted is perfectionism. This trait is a mixed blessing. On the positive side, it helps dancers excel because they set high standards and work hard to achieve their goals. The downside is that it's easy to fall into negative patterns, expecting to be perfect and making no allowances for failure. This is what happened to Tina, who fell into a common trap of all-or-nothing thinking. Either she got the job or she lacked talent: There was no middle ground. This created negative stress and anxiety, causing her to falter during auditions.

Common signs of maladaptive perfectionism include:

1. Setting unrealistically high goals that are impossible to meet

2. Being plagued by self-doubt and fear of failure

3. Feeling obsessed about making mistakes

Even successful dancers at the top of the heap have found themselves with performance anxiety. "I always had to have that perfect picture that I presented to the world," recalls principal dancer Jenifer Ringer. "When I debuted in full-length ballets I was completely stressed out. I didn't sleep and the performances were just torture. A case in point is when I did *Swan Lake* for the first time. I was sure I was going to fail miserably because I didn't know if I could look like a bird. I thought I might look silly, flapping my arms and doing the head movements. But I talked to myself the entire time, saying that it was a beautiful story and the audience could care less if I made a mistake. It worked! It was one of the best experiences I ever had and it caught me completely by surprise." Jenifer used a tried-and-true technique for performance anxiety, called "positive self-talk," which we'll discuss later in this chapter.

Coping Skills

Obviously, your ability to deal with a personally demanding situation is crucial to reducing negative stress. This is where coping skills come in handy. Edward, our ballet dancer who uses alcohol and recreational drugs to numb his fears of disappointing others, is trying to reduce stress. This need is common in perfectionists who depend on outside validation from others—a tricky situation for performers. While it's uncommon to abuse substances onstage because dancing requires fine-motor control and the ability to think on your feet, recreational drug use (after performances) affects 7 percent of dancers, according to a nationwide survey by *Dance Magazine*. Obviously, if you develop a substance abuse problem you need help. Options include twelve-step programs like Alcoholics Anonymous (www.aa.org) and Narcotics Anonymous (www.na.org), and cognitive-behavioral support groups (www.smartrecovery.org).

Healthy coping skills include good lifestyle habits (balanced meals, aerobic exercise, sufficient sleep), social support, and cognitive techniques. The American Psychological Association (www.apa.org) provides referrals to mental health specialists, if you need additional support.

The Impact of Injuries

In our study at NYCB we found that one of the most obvious indications that a dancer may be experiencing negative stress is an injury.

Athletes are taught to be tough, but the same is true for them. The American College of Sports Medicine recently issued a consensus statement informing team physicians, coaches, and athletic trainers of the link between stress and injury. Stressed-out athletes are at least twice as susceptible to injury; this includes stress related to personal problems, like breaking up with a girlfriend or boyfriend.

There are several reasons why stress increases your vulnerability to injury. Acute stress causes your attention to narrow; you may miss something in your peripheral vision and trip over a dancer or scenery or fall into the orchestra pit. Believe me, it's happened! The effect of high stress levels on your immune system also makes you more vulnerable to injury. Hard training breaks down muscle. Under normal circumstances, with adequate rest and nutrition, the body repairs itself. But stress hormones like cortisol weaken muscle tissues and impede recovery by limiting the inflammatory response that promotes healing. This increases the chances of becoming injured or a chronic problem being exacerbated. Stress also increases muscle tension. Besides affecting your coordination and throwing you off balance, tense muscles are more likely to tear.

Our last dancer, Rachel, is a prime example of a stressed-out dancer who became injured by trying to excel through overwork. She had to deal with one of the worst-case scenarios in a dancer's life—surgery! While stress may have preceded her injury, there is no doubt that it also followed it. Injuries are scary, painful, and often unpredictable. Few dancers get through this experience unscathed. In Rachel's case, it would have helped if she had responded to her friends' invitations to socialize, because this helps to mediate stress. Yet it is typical to withdraw.

Serious injuries that sideline dancers' brief careers (the average duration is a decade) create unique vulnerabilities. One of the most common reactions to being injured is depression. While the symptoms can be insidious, changes in sleeping and eating behavior are often a red flag. Abi Stafford dealt with this problem while she was recovering from her injury by going to the gym, where she did an aerobic workout (a known mood booster), using the stationary bike, to improve her frame of mind. Stress management sessions that focused on cognitive techniques, such as "reframing" her injury as an opportunity to increase her overall fitness with cross-training, provided coping skills and additional support.

How Your Body Reacts to Stress

To understand the stress response, it helps to begin with a crash course in physiology. Under threat (whether real or perceived), the brain activates the autonomic nervous system, an involuntary system of nerves that controls and stimulates the output of stress hormones. This triggers the fight-or-flight response through the sympathetic nervous system, which originates in the spinal cord and targets either muscles or glands. It also shuts down basic functions regulated by the parasympathetic nervous system, which caters to the rest-and-digest responses that conserve energy.

Known as "approach stress," your body's hormonal response to a high-stakes event will help you perform better in the following ways. First, stress hormones will enhance your cognitive ability so that you zero in on what is really important while putting your priorities in order. In other words, you will be able to respond quickly and think on your feet at the same time. Meanwhile, your immune system will kick in by fighting off colds and pain, helping you deal with demanding situations because your stress hormones, such as adrenaline, rev you up. However, if the tension is too high or too long, your body will go into overdrive.

A dancer who is under acute stress experiences various symptoms. Heart rate and respiration soar, dramatically increasing blood flow to the skeletal muscles, while diverting it from the gastrointestinal tract and skin (hence an upset stomach and cold hands and feet). In severe cases of stage fright, a dancer with an upset stomach may actually vomit before performing. Extreme stress also causes the muscles to tense, a protective reaction under perceived physical threat. Muscle tension creates backaches and headaches, while reducing flexibility, coordination, and the fine-motor control necessary to perform properly. Finally, sweat breaks out to cool the body, while the pupils dilate, allowing more light to enter the eye as attention narrows. While this reaction is useful if you're focused on a dangerous situation, it keeps dancers from noticing what's around them, making it easier to trip over scenery or someone's leg. Dancers who are hyperalert to small sounds and movements find it harder to focus on the steps and are more likely to blank out on choreography and dance combinations.

In extreme and sustained cases, the stress response can affect your self-esteem, your career goals, and even your ability to learn new skills, but luckily the audience will rarely pick up on your anxiety. Still, the key is to catch stress early and learn how to handle it properly.

Consequently, it's important to recognize the insidious stages of stress to know if you've arrived at the tipping point. A pioneer in stress research, Dr. Hans Seyle, showed that stress progresses through three stages; this is known as the General Adaption Syndrome.

1. The *alarm reaction* is characterized by the body's release of adrenaline and those nasty responses I just described. Fortunately, your body will return to normal if you remove the stressor. If not, you move into the second stage.

2. *Resistance* occurs when the body adapts to prolonged stress by secreting further hormones called corticosteroids that increase blood sugar levels to maintain energy and raise blood pressure. The body's effort to sustain arousal takes a toll. You are more prone to fatigue, irritability, burnout, weight gain, and lapses in concentration.

3. *Exhaustion* occurs when the adrenal glands can no longer meet the demands of stress. Basically, your body has run out of its reserves of energy and immunity. This leads to a host of problems, such as stress intolerance as your blood sugar levels drop, increased mental and physical exhaustion, serious illness, and eventually total collapse.

Unfortunately, some dancers, like Edward, start drinking or using drugs to combat symptoms of stress before they hit exhaustion.

They may also develop health problems, such as depression, chronic headaches, and insomnia. While we've already outlined the physical and psychological early warning signs of stress, be aware that prolonged stress may also lead to:

- Low blood sugar

- Excess pain from muscle tension

- Menstrual problems

- Intense allergic reactions

- Frequent upper-respiratory problems

The good news is that many stress-related problems are reversible. All you need are some trusty stress management strategies to counterbalance the pressures, whether internal or external. Although dancers are not typically the type to flock to lectures on how to manage stress, or seek out the latest relaxation procedure, they are highly competent and tend to respond positively to stress management sessions. Think of it as learning a new technique that will help you become a better dancer and a happier person.

The Stress-Busting Diet

Remember, there is no one magic solution to rid yourself of stress. Each person is different; also, you need different tools depending on your unique situation. You probably already have a few stress busters of your own under your belt. These may include listening to music, cooking, spending time with friends, playing with your dog, or any hobby that is not goal-directed but simply gives you pleasure. Still, going on a stress diet provides further options proven to reduce your stress level. The key is to be flexible and adaptive in dealing with the problems that you are faced with. You can and should go with the ones that work best for you, while allowing at least thirty minutes of fun time every day.

Rest and Relaxation

As you probably know by now, I am a big believer in sleep. First, too little sleep builds up stress by having a negative impact on your intellectual functioning, reaction time, and motor control. Sleep deprivation also increases appetite and adds fat to places where you would least like it, such as your stomach. Finally, dancers who fail to get eight to ten hours of sleep per night are more vulnerable to the overtraining syndrome and burnout, which occur when there is an imbalance between vigorous exercise and recovery. In contrast, sufficient sleep helps you to bounce back from intense exercise or illness, fend off depression, and maintain a healthy body weight.

Jeremy wasn't bothered by an occasional sleepless night as a contemporary dancer who liked to party. However, he noticed that overstimulation from late-night performances, TV, and time on the computer made it difficult to fall asleep when he most needed to. Power naps, while always an option, increased his insomnia. Jeremy didn't know that naps can disrupt the normal sleep cycle, throwing your circadian rhythm (the body's twenty-four-hour internal clock) out of whack. Be aware that the sleepiest part of the day is between 1:00 P.M. and 4:00 P.M. If you have trouble falling asleep at night, just say no to naps. The best remedy for a restful night is to develop good sleep rituals.

The ABCs of Catching ZZZs

Jeremy decided that he needed a plan to combat his insomnia, so he did some research on the Internet. First, he learned that certain types of drugs can cause poor sleep. These include blood pressure drugs, over-the-counter cold drugs, antidepressants, and caffeine, alcohol, and nicotine. So much for partying! He found he was better able to sleep if he backed off from caffeine by midafternoon and alcohol and nicotine late at night. In fact, he decided to quit smoking, which is associated with a host of other problems, including poor bone density.

Additionally, he found certain strategies quite useful, like going to bed and waking up around the same time every day. He also gave himself an hour to prepare for bedtime by turning down the lights (which releases the sleep-promoting hormone melatonin), shutting off the TV and computer, and adding soothing behaviors, such as reading a book, to move him from a busy workday to a feeling of calm. It helps to slow your heart rate by taking a hot bath and then stepping out and cooling yourself down (which produces a drop in body temperature), or reclining with your feet above your head. Listening to low-key music, nature sounds, or silence, depending on your preference, further reduces stress, as does deep breathing and muscle relaxation exercises (see below). Jeremy preferred silence and, like most people, found it easier to fall asleep in a cool room.

If your thoughts are whirling around all the things that you should have done during the day, switch gears by listing everything you did right. It's surprising how few high-achieving dancers ever note their accomplishments, although this wasn't Jeremy's problem. You can also relax by using imagery and deep breathing to mentally transpose yourself to your favorite place (like a Caribbean island), using all five senses to "feel" the sun, "hear" the surf, "see" the dazzling blue waters, "taste" the saltiness in the air, and "smell" the ocean to lull you to sleep. The more vivid and controllable the image, the more likely you are to relax and snooze.

Finally, dancers can prepare for sleep through progressive muscle relaxation. Jeremy liked this exercise, which was similar to the tension and relaxation series at the end of a hatha yoga class. The best time to do this is during a long break or at bedtime, *not* before a performance. Find a quiet place free from distractions. First, sequentially tense your muscles as hard as you can for five measured seconds; then relax. Follow this with a slow, deep breath and exhalation. Do each exercise twice (one at a time) in the following order: lower limbs, chest and abdomen, neck, arms and shoulders, and face. Inhale and exhale deeply after each release, while feeling the difference between the tension and the relaxation. With a little practice, you'll be asleep in no time—like Jeremy. For more details about this exercise, go to www.guidetopsychology.com/pmr.html.

Breathing

Breathing, like sleep, is essential for every dancer. However, Margot decided to use it to calm her nerves. It may seem hard to believe that something as simple as deep breathing in and out can reduce stress. Yet, with each breath, your blood absorbs and carries oxygen to every cell in your body, producing a calming effect. At the same time, exhalation removes carbon dioxide and other toxins from the body. Margot finds that deep breathing energizes her, helps her think clearly, and increases strength and flexibility. However, it takes awareness and practice. The first step is to become aware of your breath. Chest breathing (the body part that moves with each breath) is associated with being stressed out, depriving your body of oxygen. In contrast, breathing through your abdomen expands the diaphragm with this essential ingredient. Ideally, your breath should begin in your tummy, fill the middle section of your lungs, and only then reach the upper lungs. For various breathing exercises that reduce stress, increase relaxation, and reduce tension, go to www.deeplyrelax .com.

For example, five slow, deep breaths in and out can help reverse the fight-or-flight response to perceived threats, reducing anxiety, depression, irritability, and fatigue. So go for it whenever you get the chance. Megan LeCrone, who tends to get nervous before a show, has discovered the benefits. "I now do breathing exercises from yoga before a performance because of all that adrenaline." Along with her hard work to prevent further injuries, breathing has given her another tool to excel. Several weeks after her comeback, Megan was singled out in a review in *The New York Times* for her "fierce performance" in *The Four Temperaments* by George Balanchine. She has also performed difficult leading roles, as in ballets like *Agon*.

In addition to deep breathing, sitting in a relaxed position in a comfortable chair and taking a moment to reflect can also be a way to soothe yourself and reduce stress. Many dancers do this without realizing the beneficial effects. However, NYCB principal dancer Yvonne Borree says, "One of the things I've worked into my schedule is sitting down and being quiet for a few minutes each day.

We're so go-go-go that it's nice to have a quiet time as well." This is another simple stress buster that helps you let go of some of your physical anxiety by taking a few moments to sit quietly.

Meditation

A related practice that can help reduce tension and restore perspective during the day is meditation. We have all heard about the benefits, although some dancers find it difficult to sit still. Milbry decided to give it a shot after hearing her friend spout its wonders. While she was anxious at first ("What if I can't do it?"), she learned that the point of meditating is not to banish all those annoying thoughts from your mind but to notice them and let them go. It didn't matter if Milbry felt bored, angry, or frustrated. The point is, she learned to accept these thoughts and feelings without judging them. Being able to let your innermost thoughts bubble up while you sit quietly and feel the pain, and then to be able to let it go, is one route to self-acceptance and inner peace. Again, meditation may not be your first choice for stress management. Just know that relinquishing whatever might be bothering you is a good way to snap out of it, although this is easier said than done. Milbry learned that letting things go through meditation takes practice. For information about meditation at all levels of instruction, check out the World Wide Online Meditation Center at www.meditationcenter.com.

The Joy of Journals

Unlike most people, dancers often avoid journaling (along with food and stress diaries) because they don't have a lot of time to do this, especially after performing and coming home late at night. It's an alien form. Consequently, they may be unsure how a journal can help them. Yet keeping a personal log of your experiences is a fantastic way to become aware of your emotions. You feel more in control of what is going on when you put your feelings into words, making it easier to face life's challenges. The first rule of journaling is to do it only when you feel like it. It isn't meant to be a chore but can be an important way of gaining perspective. Still, this method appeals most to dancers who feel at ease verbalizing their feelings. You can do it the old-fashioned way with a pen and notebook or as a document on your computer. Your journal is there when you need it and it will not disappear, so don't feel pressured to use it all the time if you're not up to it.

"The journal writing absolutely saves me," admits corps dancer Elizabeth Walker. "It's time to reflect and focus on my emotions. The thoughts or the words swirling around distract me no longer. It's setting my perspective in order for the day." Be aware that journals may contain more than just words. You can add photos, sketches, flowers, or anything else to make a scrapbook.

Cognitive-Behavioral Therapy

This form of psychotherapy is especially attractive for dancers, as well as athletes, given that thoughts and behavior have a profound effect on performance. Research shows that it helps combat a negative body image, reduce stage fright, and improve physical skills. In fact, it is one of the top choices for elite athletes who focus on mental skills training. While there are several approaches to cognitive-behavioral therapy (CBT), most share common characteristics. For example, ballet dancer Christine discovered that her thoughts, not external situations or people, were responsible for her feelings and behaviors. This explains why dancers react differently to the same experience. The benefit was that she learned she could change the way she thinks and behaves.

CBT is also time-limited and gets results fast. The reason it's so brief is that it's highly instructive—much like taking dance class. It's also a collaborative effort between client and therapist. Christine wanted to gain self-confidence while she danced, so that became the goal. She received techniques like thought stopping (putting a rubber band on her wrist and snapping it while thinking the word "No" when she doubted herself), reframing scary thoughts (changing "I feel nervous" to "I feel up and excited"), and positive self-talk ("Don't worry about performing that ballet. You've done it before and you can do it again") to counter negative thinking with facts, logic, and reason. Her therapist's role was to listen, teach, and encourage her to reach her goal. Christine was also able to express her concerns, learn a lot, and put what she knew into practice because she trusted her therapist.

Casey is a twenty-one-year-old modern dancer who also decided to give CBT a try. Her major problem involved giving up whenever she felt insecure, because she only had four years of training under her belt. In spite of her natural talent, small snubs by her teachers or missteps in class unleashed a flood of negative emotions. Casey agreed to keep a stress diary to record her negative thoughts and counter them on a daily basis.

A stress diary can help you identify automatic thoughts based on your beliefs that affect mood and behavior. Examples of dysfunctional thinking in dancers include:

- Regarding mistakes in a class, audition, or performance as a sign of total failure

- Interpreting ambiguous reactions from others as negative without enough evidence

- Highlighting the importance of errors while downplaying your accomplishments

- Believing that negative feelings about yourself are accurate ("I have no talent")

Not surprisingly, such thinking affects your mood and behavior. The good news is that you can challenge these beliefs by keeping a daily record of upsetting situations, the resulting negative thoughts or images, and a rational response to counter them. Casey's instructions were to write down an automatic thought or image that preceded a negative emotion and the situation that triggered it, and then counter it with a rational response. To work, she needs to believe it. So she uses an easy technique to find the right words by imagining what she'd say to her friend in the same situation.

Casey then takes a Graham class—one of her favorites. Halfway through the class she notices that her mood has plummeted and she wants to give up. She writes the following entry after class.

Casey's Stress Diary

STRESSFUL SITUATION	AUTOMATIC THOUGHT/IMAGE	RATIONAL RESPONSE
My teacher ignored me when I did a really hard dance step across the room.	"She hates my dancing. If I'm that bad, why even try the next step. I'll just sit down."	"Give yourself a break! You did a tough step without stopping. That's what matters."

Lack of attention from her teacher triggers feelings of insecurity that make Casey want to retreat. She dutifully notes the situation and automatic thoughts, but her mind goes blank when it comes to using positive self-talk to counter them with a rational response. Casey decides to imagine what she would say to her best friend if she were in her shoes. Suddenly, she knows what to say to herself, and this gives her perspective. It's not the end of her career if a teacher doesn't pay attention to how she executes one step. She subsequently feels better and does the next combination.

By distancing herself from her negative thoughts, Casey is able to look at a potentially stressful situation objectively without personalizing it. She can see that becoming upset does not do her any good. She had done her best and there was no reason to assume otherwise. So she uses facts, logic, and reason to cope with her negative reaction and turn it around.

Jenifer Ringer also benefited by using positive self-talk to counter her negative thoughts about being a swan, making it one of the most exhilarating experiences of her life onstage. When all is said and done, it is the perception of danger that leads to the stress response. Appendix I provides a blank stress diary that you can copy and use. Even if you catch one negative thought a day, you're well on your way to developing more adaptive ways to deal with stress.

Decompressing

All dancers can also use a commonsense list to work downtime into their schedule. An imbalance between exercise and recovery can lead to a full-blown case of overtraining and burnout. This can occur whether you are performing several ballets a night, doing the same Broadway show every week, or dancing five or more hours a day in a summer intensive course.

The most obvious sign of the overtraining syndrome is when your performance deteriorates for no apparent reason. Suddenly, your technique is off, old mistakes reappear, you can't concentrate, and you are forgetting new steps. The tendency at this stage is to work harder to compensate, but overwork is the problem, *not* the solution. Emotional and physical exhaustion can lead to a severe case of burnout and it can take six to twelve weeks of rest to recover, so the best line of defense is prevention. Here is what you can do.

1. Set aside one day each week for a "personal day" to do whatever makes you feel happy and relaxed, as long as it does not involve working out. Twenty-four hours of very little physical activity helps you recover from vigorous exercise, leading to improvements in power, strength, and endurance.

2. Ease into an upcoming performance season or class schedule by getting fit a month ahead of time through strength training, aerobics, and technique class. Dancing yourself into shape is not an option. All it does is increase your chance of overtraining and burnout.

3. Fight off upper-respiratory infections by eating a well-balanced diet with adequate amounts of carbohydrates, fat, and protein to boost your immune system. A multivitamin with essential minerals will also help ward off illness from intense exercise.

4. Do not dance with a serious illness like mononucleosis or a chronic injury. A no pain, no gain attitude usually backfires.

5. Allow sufficient time to sleep to help your body recover from excessive exercise. While ten hours may seem impossible to achieve, it improves memory, mood, stress level, and healing time from injuries.

Remember to add weekly regenerative activities to your regime even if you are a student—saunas, massage, whirlpools, or aromatherapy.

For some, it may seem like a supreme indulgence, but it is important to take care of your body and mind.

In Summary

By now, I hope you know that stress is part of life. If you are experiencing a lot of stress, chances are you are a highly competent person who has not yet learned to say no to that self-critical voice inside. Not to worry. Change takes time, but you should not ignore the warning signs telling you that enough is enough. Listen to yourself. There are many ways to deal with stress, and the choice is up to you how you will handle it. You are not alone.

PART THREE

Resources

Books, DVDs, Web Sites, and More

Dance Attire and Equipment

- Bunheads (www.bunheads.com): A range of innovative dance accessories, including toe ribbons with elastics (flexors) to combat tendonitis and special products for foot protection.

- Danskin (www.danskin.com/nycb-logoessentials-6938.html): Fun, attractive, comfortable attire with New York City Ballet logos.

- NuMetrex (www.numetrex.com): Sports bras and shirts that measure heart rate with a built-in monitor and a stopwatch to assess aerobic fitness.

- Fancyfoot Arch Enhancer (www.fancyfoot.com): Specially designed instep pads that slip on top of the foot to enhance the line in the pointed position.

- Alternative Soles (www.alternativesoles.com): Ballet and tap shoes for vegetarians, which use no animal products.

- JAM (www.jamcosmetics.net): An online store that provides cosmetics and instruction on how to use makeup specially formulated for dancers.

- J. Barringer and S. Schlesinger, *The Pointe Book: Shoes, Training, & Technique,* 2nd ed. (Hightstown, NJ: Princeton Book Company, 2004): An in-depth book about pointe shoes, available through Dance Horizons (www.dancehorizons.com).

- "When Can I Start Pointe Work?": An informative resource article regarding toe work, available through IADMS (www .iadms.org).

- Judy Rice, *Tricks of the Trade* and *Pointe Work: The Next Step:* DVDs illustrating the best ways to get the most out of your toe shoes, for everyone from beginners to advanced-level dancers, and a basic pointe-work barre, available at www.behindbarres.com.

- American Harlequin Corporation (www.harlequinfloors.com): High-quality flooring options for studio and stage.

- Macfadden Performing Arts Media publications: *Dance Magazine, Pointe, Dance Spirit,* and *Dance Teacher* (www.macfadden .dancemedia.com/subscribe).

Cross-Training

- E. Franklin, *Conditioning for Dance: Training for Peak Performance in All Dance Forms* (Champaign, IL: Human Kinetics, 2004): A comprehensive book on conditioning exercises that apply to all forms of dance (www.humankinetics.com).

- B. Anderson, *Stretching,* rev. ed. (Berkeley, CA: Shelter Publications, 2000): A highly descriptive book on stretching different parts of the body (www.shelterpub.com).

- International Association for Dance Medicine & Science, "The Challenge of the Adolescent Dancer" (www.iadms.org): Resource paper about how to avoid exercise-related problems during growth spurts.

- Hypermobility Syndrome Association (www.hypermobility .org): Information and support regarding problems associated with extreme hypermobility.

- Jason R. Karp, "Muscle Fiber Types and Training" (www .coachr.org/fiber.htm): An excellent summary on altering body build.

- National Athletic Trainers in the Performing Arts (search for atc_performingarts group at http://health.groups.yahoo.com): For referrals.

- Gyrotonic Expansion System (www.gyrotonic.com): For referrals.

- Yoga for Dancers (www.hilarycartwright.com): For information about classes in NYC and workshops.

- Yoga Alliance (www.yogaalliance.org): For referrals.

- Pilates (www.pmapilatescertified.com): For referrals.

Dance Medicine Education and Referrals

- *Introduction to Dance Medicine: Keeping Dancers Dancing* and *Lower Extremities.* VHS. Produced by Susan Macaluso (New York: Dance Medicine Education Fund, 1992; updated for DVD format in 2006): Features NYCB orthopedist Dr. William Hamilton, in collaboration with NYCB physical therapists Marika Molnar and Katy Keller; call to order at 718-426-8606.

- International Association for Dance Medicine & Science (www.iadms.org): The Executive Director provides ad hoc referrals to dance medicine specialists, with plans by the board to produce a dance medicine resource guide in the future. (IADMS membership includes discounts to periodicals and annual conferences.)

- American Academy of Orthopedic Surgeons (www.orthoinfo.org): For referrals.

- American Orthopedic Foot & Ankle Society (www.aofas.org): For referrals.

- American Physical Therapy Association (www.apta.org): For referrals.

- American Massage Therapy Association (www.amtamassage .org): For referrals.

- American Psychological Association (www.apa.org): For referrals.

- American Council on Exercise (www.acefitness.org): Home-study certification for survival jobs.

- Career Transition for Dancers (www.careertransition.org): Provides students and professionals with resources to develop other interests and skills to prepare for life after dance.

Eating Disorders

- Eating Attitudes Test (EAT-26) (www.sa.psu.edu/uhs/health information/eatingattitudes.cfm): Provides feedback about concerns and attitudes that may warrant further evaluation.

- Renfrew Center (www.renfrewcenter.com/for-family-friends/ index.asp): First U.S. residential eating disorder program focused on women's issues. Provides a nationwide referral network of health-care providers, as well as practical advice about how to help a friend or family member with an eating disorder.

- J. Schaefer and T. Rutledge, *Life Without Ed* (New York: McGraw-Hill, 2004): An inspirational book that equates recovering from an eating disorder ("Ed") with leaving an abusive relationship.

- *Dying to Be Thin*. VHS/DVD. Produced by NOVA, 2000: The story of dancers, models, and others recovering from eating disorders. Available at www.pbs.org/wgbh/nova/thin/. An adapted version for teachers who work with students in grades nine to twelve is also available.

- Eating Disorder Referral and Information Center (www .edreferral.com): For information about local support groups, health-care professionals, treatment centers, and choosing credentialed providers.

- Overeaters Anonymous (www.overeatersanonymous.org): Twelve-step support groups with local and online meetings.

Health Care and Insurance

- Boston Women's Health Book Collective and Judy Norsigian, *Our Bodies, Ourselves: A New Edition for a New Era* (New York: Touchstone, 2005): Five-star reference book on women's physical and mental health.

- Emergency Fund for Student Dancers (www.efsdancers.org): Information about health insurance and service providers, plus emergency loans for full-time students at specified dance schools.

- The Dancers' Resource: the Actors Fund's program that provides services to injured professional dancers. It includes one-on-one counseling, seminars and workshops, resources and referrals in such areas as mental health care, health-care access, health insurance counseling, injury support, and emergency financial assistance. It also serves as a gateway for dancers to access the Fund's many other supportive programs. For more information, visit www.actorsfund.org.

- ArtistAccess: Health care in exchange for artistic services (for example, entertaining a group of hospital patients); contact Woodhull Medical and Mental Health Center, Brooklyn, New York (www.nyfa.org/files_uploaded/healthfaqs.pdf).

- National Association of Public Hospitals (www.naph.org): Information about high-quality health-care services available at city hospitals for patients who lack sufficient insurance, regardless of their ability to pay.

- Al Hirschfeld Free Health Clinic: Free primary care services in New York for qualified uninsured or underinsured members of the entertainment industry; contact the Actors Fund of America (www.actorsfund.org).

- Access to Health Insurance/Resources for Care (www.ahirc.org): For information nationwide about affordable health-care services and insurance for artists.

- The Entertainment Industry Group Insurance Trust (www.teigit.com): For artists affiliated with various professional associations, such as the American Guild of Musical Artists.

- Workers' Compensation, U.S. Department of Labor (www.dol.gov/esa): For job-related injuries; information about filing a claim to help pay medical bills and compensate for lost salary.

Nutrition

- International Association for Dance Medicine & Science, "Nutrition Fact Sheet: Fueling the Dancer" (www.iadms.org).

- Safe food: For government information on food safety, including the mercury content in fish, call 1-888-SAFEFOOD.

- American Dietetic Association (www.eatright.org): For referrals.

- Consumer Lab (www.consumerlab.com): For a nominal fee, get the latest on vitamins, supplements, etc.

- BPA-free products (www.ewg.org/node/20999): For information on minimizing exposure to bisphenol A until final FDA conclusions.

- Hannaford's "Guiding Stars" awards three stars to the healthiest foods in supermarkets; available at www.hannaford.com.

- HydraTrend strips (www.medco-athletics.com): For all accurate assessment of hydration.

- Online calorie counter (www.thecaloriecounter.com): Nutrition data on different foods, including restaurant and take-out dishes.

- N. Goldbeck and D. Goldbeck, *Healthy Highways: The Traveler's Guide to Healthy Eating* (Woodstock, NY: Ceres Press, 2004): Information about the healthiest restaurants and natural food stores in all fifty states (www.healthyhighways.com).

Stress Management

- Stress tests (www.lessons4living.com): Personal feedback about stress, burnout, and depression.

- Self-esteem (www.positive-way.com/self-est1.htm): Questionnaire and information on self-esteem.

- Muscle relaxation (www.guidetopsychology.com/pmr.htm): Detailed description from psychologist Dr. Raymond Lloyd Richmond.

- Breathing exercises (www.stress.about.com): For techniques to reduce stress and tension and to increase relaxation.

- H. Benson, with M. Z. Klipper, *The Relaxation Response* (New York: HarperCollins, 2000): A classic book on stress reduction.

- M. E. Seligman, *Learned Optimism: How to Change Your Mind and Your Life* (New York: Vintage Books, 2006): A book on the power of optimism.

- World Wide Online Meditation Center (www.meditation center.com): Information about meditation at all levels of instruction.

- Insomnia (www.mayoclinic.com/health/insomniaDS00187): Prevent insomnia through sleep rituals and by avoiding certain ingredients, prescription medications, over-the-counter cold drugs, and nicotine.

Substance Abuse

- Do It Now Foundation (www.doitnow.org/pages/pubhub
.html): Brochures about alcohol, drugs, smoking and kids.

- Addiction Resource Guide (www.addictionresourceguide
.com): Guidelines for choosing a rehabilitation program.

- J. O. Prochaska, J. Norcross, and C. DiClemente, *Changing for
Good* (New York: HarperCollins, 1994): Negotiating the stages
of change.

- P. Fanning and J. T. O'Neill, *The Addiction Workbook: A Step-
by-Step Guide to Quitting Alcohol and Drugs* (Oakland, CA: New
Harbinger, 1996): A comprehensive workbook.

- Alcoholics Anonymous (www.aa.org) and Narcotics Anonymous (www.na.org): National support groups using the twelve-
step program.

- Smart Recovery (www.smartrecovery.org): National support
groups using a cognitive-behavioral approach to abstinence.

- Nicotine Anonymous World Services (www.nicotine-
anonymous.org): National support groups dealing with smoking addiction.

- Quit Net (www.quitnet.com): An online support site provided by people who have stopped smoking.

Weight Management

- Basal metabolic rate (www.gymgoal.com/dtool_bmr.html):
Calculate the Harris–Benedict BMR.

- Body mass index (www.bariatricedge.com): Calculate BMI.

- B. Wansink, *Mindless Eating: Why We Eat More Than We Think* (New York: Bantam Books, 2006): A thorough review of the triggers that sabotage weight management and sensible solutions (www.randomhouse.com/bantamdell).

Dance Medicine Glossary

BY WILLIAM G. HAMILTON, M.D.

Anatomical Positions

abduction: away from the midline of the body
adduction: toward the midline of the body
cephalad: toward the head
caudad or caudal: toward the tail
superior: above
inferior: below
supine: faceup
prone: facedown
proximal: nearer
distal: farther

Injury Definitions

acute injuries: occur suddenly, often after a slip or fall
chronic injuries: involve ongoing symptoms
fracture or break: a crack in the structure of the bone
hairline fracture: undisplaced and sometimes hard to see on an
    x-ray until it begins to heal three weeks later
inflammation: pain, heat, swelling, redness, and tenderness in a body
    part, such as a muscle, tendon, or joint
shin splint: localized pain in the leg where a muscle attaches to the
    tibia or shinbone

spondylosis: degeneration of the spine

sprain: a partial or complete tear of a ligament that holds a joint together; severity is graded according to the amount of damage: grade 1, a small tear; grade 2, a significant but incomplete tear; grade 3, a complete tear

strains or pulls: some or all of the fibers in a weak or tight muscle are torn; damage is graded as mild (grade 1), moderate (grade 2), or severe (grade 3)

stress fracture: a break that results from repetitive overload

stress reaction: precursor to a stress fracture that is slowly worsening

tendonitis: an inflamed tendon, which is the inelastic structure that connects a muscle to a bone

Common Problems in Specific Areas

The Ankle

Achilles tendon rupture: a very serious injury, usually in an older male dancer; recovery takes one year

Achilles tendonitis: pain and swelling in the Achilles tendon itself or in its insertion into the heel bone; usually occurs after a strain or overuse of the tendon

ankle sprain: an injury to one of the two main ligaments that stabilize the lateral (outside) ankle when the foot is twisted inward; the most common acute injury in sports and dancing, graded 1 (partial tear to one ligament), 2 (complete tear of one ligament), or 3 (complete tear of both ligaments)

dancer's tendonitis: tendonitis of the flexor hallucis longus (FHL) tendon; pain and swelling in the tendon to the great toe that runs down the inside of the ankle; occurs primarily in dancers who work on pointe

high ankle sprain: sprain on the outside of the ankle above the usual sprain; takes much longer to heal than a regular sprain

posterior impingement: pinching between the bones in the back of the ankle when rising onto pointe or demi-pointe; usually caused by an extra bone, called the os trigonum. It is sometimes difficult to tell the difference between posterior impingement and FHL tendonitis because they can coexist.

The Calf

muscle strain or pull: usually happens in the medial (inside) muscle of the calf; ranges from mild to severe; common in tennis players and is sometimes called "tennis leg"

Elbows, Wrists, and Hands

fractures: usually occur as a result of falling from a lift
tendonitis: usually occurs as a result of overuse

The Foot

bunion: deformity in the big toe or first metatarsophalangeal (MP) joint; a large bump forms on the medial side of the joint and the great toe drifts toward the second toe. Serious dancers should not have surgery on this problem until they retire because the operation will often result in stiffness and loss of the demi-pointe relevé.
hallux rigidus: stiffening of the first MP joint in the big toe from early arthritis in the joint. It is painful and interferes with the relevé.
Morton's neuroma: pinched nerve in the foot, usually between the third and fourth toes. It causes stinging pain that radiates into the toes and gets better when the shoes are removed and the toes are massaged.
stress fracture: common in dancers; often occurs at the base of the second metatarsal (the long bone in the forefoot that runs to the second toe); easily diagnosed by localized pain and tenderness

The Hip

iliopsoas tendonitis: strain of the large tendon that runs down the front of the hip, causing groin pain with a passé

painful turnout: Rotation of the hip (the bony ball-and-socket joint that allows rotation, flexion, and extension) is determined genetically, not by exercise. People are born with three configurations in their hips: anteverted (pigeon-toed, or turned in), normal (equally turned in and turned out), and retroverted (duck-footed, or turned out). Unfortunately, dancers who are born anteverted will never gain enough turnout to do serious ballet no matter how hard they work at it. Forcing turnout can damage the hip socket and lead to arthritis and injury to the knee. It is very important that dancers simply work with the turnout that Mother Nature gave them and not try to gain perfect turnout when they don't have it.

torn labrum: tear in the cartilaginous rim on the edge of the hip socket; often occurs as a result of forced turnout, causing pain and snapping in the groin

The Knee

dislocating kneecap: usually occurs in loose-jointed dancers. When the kneecap, or patella, slips out and goes back in place by itself, it is called a subluxation; weak muscles, poor technique, and turning out below the knee contribute to this injury. Dislocation requires an emergency visit to the hospital to put it back in place.

jumper's knee: tendonitis of the tendon beneath the kneecap, or patella; usually the result of overuse and common in male dancers who jump a lot

torn cartilage: tear in the tough, rubbery cartilage, or meniscus, two crescent-shaped structures within the knee that provide cushioning and shock absorption. When they are damaged or torn they can irritate the knee, causing pain and swelling; if they are fragmented, they can catch in the knee and cause locking.

torn anterior cruciate ligament (ACL): a tear in the ligament in the knee joint that provides stability; the knee tends to buckle or give way with certain movements. This injury is much more common in contact sports such as football or soccer than in dancing.

torn medial collateral ligament (MCL): an injury to the ligament on the medial (inside) of the knee; graded according to level of severity: grade 1 (small partial tear); grade 2 (significant partial tear); and grade 3 (complete tear). A grade 3 injury of this ligament is often associated with other injuries, such as a torn anterior cruciate ligament.

The Lower Back

Pain in the lower back, or lumbar spine, is usually due to one, or a combination, of the following:

muscle strain or pull: usually causes localized pain and spasm that may radiate into the buttock but not down the leg; very common

slipped or herniated disc: characterized by pain down the leg, with attendant numbness, tingling, and weakness (sciatica). The resilient discs between each vertebra have a soft center like a donut and act as shock absorbers. If overloaded, this center can protrude, or herniate, through the rim, pressing against a nerve that runs down the back of the leg.

spondylolisthesis: a serious condition caused by stress fractures on both sides of the lower spine that allow a vertebra to slip forward on the one below

stress fracture or spondylolysis: characterized by recurrent or persistent but nonradiating unilateral (one side only) back pain that occurs with an arabesque on the affected side. It is caused by repeated extreme movements, such as arabesques, attitudes, battements, and port des bras. A bone scan will confirm this.

The Midback

dorsolumbar back strains: common in the midback of male dancers when lifting or partnering; often due to weakness in the shoulders and arms

rib fractures: often occur when a female dancer is being lifted and the hand of her partner jams into the lower rib cage

The Neck

pinched nerves and arthritis: characterized by pain in the cervical spine that radiates down the arm; usually associated with arthritis in older dancers

strains: nonradiating pain and stiffness with inability to move the neck through a full range of motion

The Shin

compartment syndrome: pain in the shin (large long bone below the knee) that more commonly results from sustained activities like running and soccer, rather than dancing; caused by the muscles of the leg swelling within their tight sheaths and choking off their own blood supply

shin splints: similar to stress fractures but they occur over a broader area, usually three fingerwidths rather than one; caused by a strain of an area where a muscle attaches to the shinbone, or tibia

stress fracture: common in male dancers who jump a lot, usually in the front, but occasionally in the back of the bone; if a painful lump forms on the bone that can be felt with one finger, it is likely to be a stress fracture. A bone scan will confirm this.

The Shoulders

dislocations and subluxations: common in very loose-jointed dancers, especially males who need to lift when partnering

fractures: these are very rare; they may occur when someone is dropped from a lift

stress fractures of the first rib: occur in teenage male dancers who go to the gym and do excessive weight lifting

Practitioners

All practitioners have to pass various certification or licensing examinations.

athletic trainer (A.T.C.): college graduate specially trained in the treatment of acute and chronic musculoskeletal injuries; usually part of an athletic team

certified dietician (C.D.N.): has academic and supervised experience in nutrition education and counseling

chiropractor (D.C.): graduate of chiropractic school, trained in the conservative treatment of musculoskeletal problems

clinical psychologist (Ph.D.): has a doctorate in psychology and postgraduate training and supervision in psychotherapy

clinical social worker (M.S.W.): has a master's degree in social work and completed postgraduate supervision and training in psychotherapy

medical doctor (M.D.): has a medical degree and has completed an internship to be a general practitioner; specialties such as surgery, internal medicine, and psychiatry require further training beyond internship

orthopedist or orthopedic surgeon (M.D.): a medical doctor who treats and operates upon injuries to the musculoskeletal system (bones, joints, muscles, tendons)

osteopath (D.O.): equivalent of a medical doctor

physical therapist (P.T.): treats and rehabilitates injuries by hands-on methods, often under the supervision of an M.D.; usually have master's or doctoral degrees and are part of a team of health-care providers

podiatrist (D.P.M.): graduate of podiatry school (not medical school); treats disorders of the foot

psychiatrist (M.D.): medical doctor with postgraduate training for mental disorders; can prescribe medication and may or may not choose to do psychotherapy

registered dietician (R.D.): has passed a rigorous registration exam (unlike other nutrition counselors) after postgraduate training

Types of Medical Tests

bone scan: performed to look for something in the bone that does not show on anything else. It actually measures increased blood flow in a specific area. It is very accurate and shows such things as unrecognized fractures and stress fractures, early arthritis, and bone tumors or bone infections.

computerized axial tomography (CAT): CAT scan is used to look more closely at the bony structures.

magnetic resonance imaging (MRI): MRI is a more complicated and expensive study done to examine the soft tissues and look for things that may not show on a regular x-ray. A hip coil is an added piece of equipment that gives you better definition, necessary to identify a labral tear.

x-ray: a simple study done to visualize the bones and see if there is an obvious fracture or other problem. Soft tissues such as muscles and tendons will not show on an x-ray.

Orthopedic Screening

Dr. William Hamilton developed this simple exam to identify minor orthopedic problems in dance that can often lead to problems if left unaddressed. The dancer first fills out a health, training, and injury history questionnaire (shown at the end of this section). The physical exam uses several ballet positions because most dancers study this technique. Health-care professionals who wish to employ Dr. Hamilton's exam should follow the procedure outlined below. Explanations of medical terms and the reason for making specific assessments are included for those who might like to be screened.

Overall, the practitioner examines the patient in the following positions:

1. Standing for general physical parameters, leg lengths, and relevé, and, when bending forward, for scoliosis

2. Prone (lying facedown) for hip motion, turnout, and the presence of a slipped vertebra (spondylolisthesis) or after a stress fracture (spondylolysis)

3. Supine (lying faceup) for the hip and hamstrings

4. Sitting over the edge of the table for the knee, foot, and ankle

Leg Length

Everyone is asymmetrical somewhere. However, if one of your legs is more than half an inch shorter than the other, it can create back pain. This difference may develop from a curved back, unequal leg lengths, or a combination of both. Your practitioner will look at you in the standing position from behind to determine if your pelvis is level or tilted. If it is not level and you have back problems, a heel lift inserted in your shoe can often help.

Scoliosis

A spinal curve in a young person (ages ten to twelve) is genetic and needs to be followed carefully by a scoliosis specialist to keep it from getting worse. Many dancers and athletes with a delay in puberty develop small curves of no significance in their late teens, simply because their backs are still growing. These curves are permanent but usually cause no symptoms. When trying to spot scoliosis, the practitioner will ask you to bend forward from the standing position, with your upper body parallel to the floor. This will allow the contour of your rib cage to show from behind. If needed, your practitioner may correct for leg length inequality during the exam by putting a lift under the heel of your shorter leg. Scoliosis shows up when your rib cage is higher on one side because of the curvature. While a mild curve is barely detectable, this is not true for moderate or severe scoliosis, which requires bracing with exercises or even surgery.

Flexibility

Tightness can lead to injuries like muscle pulls. Several years of dancing should allow you to bend over with straight legs and place your palms to the floor. If you are unable to do this, it means that your back and hamstrings are tight. A supervised stretching program is the proper way to correct the problem. Trying to increase flexibility by forcing your body or overstretching it in "hot" yoga is not the answer.

Axial Alignment

This term refers to the shape of your legs. Some people's legs are straight; others are bowed (which makes it easier to close in fifth position). If you are knock-kneed, it will be difficult to stand in either a good parallel or a turnout position. Forcing it is not going to help. Instead, it is best to work within your natural limitations. You do not need a perfect fifth position to be a beautiful dancer.

Knee Hyperextension

The other potential problem is excessive hyperextension of the knees. Your practitioner will ask you to stand with your feet together (parallel) while he or she examines your knees from the front. Dancers normally have 10 to 15 degrees of hyperextension. If you are loose-jointed, you may have more than that, and exercises such as quad and hamstring strengthening can help prevent potential knee injuries. If they appear straight, but as you shift into excessive hyperextension they become more bowed, the term "pseudo-bowed" is used.

First Position

Doing a grand plié where the knees are bent parallel to first position (heels together with feet turned out, ideally 180 degrees) is a great way to assess your arch and the depth of your plié. High arches create a shallow plié, whereas any asymmetry indicates that something is keeping one ankle from being able to complete its full range of motion. In both cases, the best approach when dancing is to let your heels go up to create the illusion of a deep plié. If you roll in (pronate) while doing a grand plié, you are probably trying to force your turnout. A much better remedy is to strengthen the tiny turnout muscles in your hips through physical therapy and cross-conditioning exercises.

Second Position

Rising to demi-pointe in second position (feet turned out, shoulder-width apart) requires the use of the whole foot and ankle. This is the best way to tell how good your pointe position really is, because you cannot force it to go up higher than you can in this position. While there is no magic answer for a poor pointe, working correctly by keeping your foot directly under you helps. The same goes for trying to achieve turnout without rolling in. "Sickling" occurs on demi-pointe (excess weight on the outside of your foot) when you are weak or lack technique, both of which can be fixed by working with correct ballet placement.

Fifth Position

Ballet's fifth position (feet turned out and crossed over heel-to-toe) determines the quality of your turnout. Your practitioner is looking for symmetry (one leg may have more turnout than another as you switch feet) and pronation (rolling in) to fake it. The only way to improve turnout is by working the tiny muscles that help you achieve your potential within your bony structures (hip sockets and knees, which cannot be altered). If you force it, you are likely to get injured.

Sauté Three Times

The best way to test for strength and placement is jumping in first position. Your practitioner will ask you to jump three times on one foot in this position. Rolling in, weak takeoffs, and hard landings are all signs of weakness and poor placement that need to be corrected by strengthening exercises and technique corrections.

Lumbosacral Step-off (Spondylolisthesis)

Sometimes, growing dancers push too hard with their leg extensions while their bones are still weak. The result can be a stress fracture in the lower back. The telltale sign is pain on one side of your back during an arabesque (one leg lifted ninety degrees to the back) but not on the other side. Unfortunately, many dancers choose to ignore this. After all, most of us have a high tolerance for pain. But if you continue to dance, the bones will be unable to heal normally. Instead, you may end up with scar tissue or a slipped vertebra, often called a "step-off," which your practitioner can feel by examining the area in your lower back. There is nothing you can do at this point aside from keeping your abdominals strong and backing off from strenuous activities when it is symptomatic. Believe it or not, Saran Wrap covering your lower back can help by providing moist heat, much like a (moist) heating pad, to keep the muscles from going into spasm. Of course, the best approach is to see an orthopedist as soon as your back hurts. If you pick up a stress fracture early, a back brace can immobilize it until it heals.

Hip Motion

The best way to judge turnout is to examine hip motion when you are lying facedown with your legs straight and together. Your practitioner will raise each foot toward the ceiling, placing a hand on your lower back to stabilize you while turning each leg inward across your other leg (turnout), then outward (turn-in). Your right and left sides are not always the same. About 50 percent of dancers have equal motion in both hips, but the other half do not.

Next, the practitioner will bend both of your feet up toward the ceiling with the heels touching and turn them to the side (like a frog) to see the turnout from the knees down. Again this may not be the same on both sides of the body. Being aware of the quality of your turnout lets you know just how much this can be safely pushed.

Quadriceps Tightness

While you are lying facedown, it is possible to check for tightness of the quadriceps muscles that run down the front of the thigh to the kneecap. This is done by trying to bend both knees so the heels reach the buttocks. If the quads are tight, this may be difficult to do. However, dancers often have well-developed hamstring muscles in the back of the legs that may hinder this motion simply because of the bulk of the muscles. A dance medicine specialist can tell the difference and put you on a stretching regimen. Dancers rarely have tight quadriceps muscles because they are usually flexible.

Hamstring Tightness

The easiest way to spot tight hamstrings is to lie on your back while the practitioner places a hand under your heel and moves the straight leg up and toward your head while the other leg rests on the table. The minimum motion is ninety degrees upward for men, but it should be higher for women. If your hamstrings are tight, there is a much greater chance that you could pull or strain them. This is a bad injury. Not only does it take a long time to heal, but a strain can form tight scar tissue during the healing process, making it prone to reinjury. The best remedy is prevention. This tightness is one of the most important things to pick up on the exam. Physical therapy can teach you safe ways to stretch your hamstrings so that you don't become injured, and can also treat scar tissue.

Hip Flexion-Adduction Sign

The hip socket has a small lip of cartilage attached to its rim, called the labrum, which can be torn by forcing turnout. This injury can cause pain in the groin that resembles tendonitis, except it does not go away. An accurate test for this problem is to pull the knee up (flexion of the hip) while lying down on your back and move it toward the midline of the body (adduction). If this is painful, your labrum may be torn. The good news is that many of these labral injuries go away with time and physical therapy. While they heal, it is important to work within the limits of discomfort (don't do what hurts).

Patellar Malalignment

Sitting on the side of a table with your legs dangling is a good position for the rest of the exam. The first of these is patellar malalignment. This refers to how the kneecap (patella) "tracks" or moves up and down in its groove on the end of the thigh bone. If it deviates (moves outward) or grinds as it moves, it may cause you problems down the road. In some cases, the motion may feel scary, as though the kneecap is slipping out of place (subluxation). This is called the "apprehension sign" by orthopedists. The good news is that strengthening exercises can often keep it on track, while preventing a possible torn ligament. Dancers with this condition should be very careful not to get their turnout from below the knee, because it makes this problem much worse and they risk dislocating their kneecap.

Patellar Tendonitis

There is a short tendon that connects the kneecap to the shinbone below, the infra patellar tendon. Jumping on hard floors or general overuse can strain it, causing it to hurt even when you're not dancing. Dancers with this tendonitis, referred to as "jumper's knee," have a characteristically tender spot on this tendon just below the kneecap. Modified activities, avoiding jumping and grand pliés, while getting a regimen of physical therapy can help.

Ankle Plantar Flexion

The last part of the orthopedic exam focuses on the foot and ankle. The dancer moves the foot into the pointe position, which allows the practitioner to see if the motion is the same in both ankles. If one foot does not point as much as the other, there may be an extra bone in the back of the ankle, the os trigonum, blocking the downward movement of the foot. The next test determines whether this extra bone is also a source of pain.

The Plantar Flexion Sign

In the pointe position the practitioner forces the ankles downward to see if this movement hurts in the back of the ankle. Pain is a sign of posterior impingement, or pinching in the back of the ankle. Treatment rarely involves surgery if you can quiet the inflammation by avoiding things that hurt. Stop trying to improve your pointe by asking your friends to sit on your foot!

Subtalar Motion

You have two ankle joints. The main one moves up and down, while the bottom joint beneath it moves side to side. You use the bottom one while walking on uneven ground like cobblestones or the side of a hill. Referred to as the subtalar joint, it plays an important role in normal foot and ankle mechanics. As a result, anything that limits this motion can cause many problems. This part of the exam checks to see if the inward-outward motion of the heel in the dangling foot is normal in both ankles by comparing one to the other. If the motion is unequal or decreased, you may need further evaluation and possible treatment.

The Drawer Sign

Ankle sprains tend to recur because they stretch out the ligaments that hold the bones of the joint together, leaving you with a permanently loose ankle. This test checks for laxity or looseness in the ankle ligaments by stabilizing the leg with one hand and pulling the ankle forward (like a drawer) with the other. The looseness comes in varying degrees and usually responds well to physical therapy. It is not painful if done when the ankle is asymptomatic.

Peroneal Weakness

There are two important peroneal tendons that run down the outside of the ankle. The strength of these tendons helps prevent the ankle from rolling inward. This part of the exam checks to see if they are strong by holding the pointe position of the foot against applied inward resistance. Well-conditioned dancers or athletes should be able to resist as much force as the practitioner uses. If the peroneal tendons give way, they require special strengthening exercises supervised by a physical therapist to prevent a potential ankle sprain.

Foot Type

Dancers have many different foot types. The Grecian (or Morton's) foot where the second toe is the longest; the Egyptian foot with a long great toe; the Giselle (or peasant) foot that is broad and square—ideal for a dancer; the simian foot that forms a bunion; and the model's foot, which is narrow and tapered—nice to look at but poor for dancing. It is important to know how to work with your foot type to protect yourself from possible injuries. A qualified practitioner can help you out by making suggestions like those outlined in Chapter 5.

Arch Type

The arch is the hollow area under the sole of the foot. There are three arch types: normal, flat, and high, or cavus. Although people inherit one type or other, dance training can help mold your foot until it stops growing around age thirteen to fourteen. Be aware that while a cavus foot provides the right look on relevé, it has a shallow plié and is prone to stress fractures because it absorbs energy poorly. Special exercises for extra strength and modifying technique such as allowing the heels to rise early in the plié can help.

Recommendations

This is the most important part of the annual orthopedic exam. Your practitioner will help you identify areas that can be corrected by physical therapy. Remember, prevention is best, so try to get screened *before* an injury occurs.

Included in this appendix are the forms used in the orthopedic assessment: The first one is filled out by the dancer and the second is used by the doctor.

Confidential Health, Training, and Injury History

Name:_____ Age:_____ DOB:__/__/____ Sex: M/F

Local address:_____ Local phone: (___)___-____

Home address:_____ Home phone: (___)___-_____

Next of kin (relation): _____

Address: _____ Home phone: (___)___-_____

Allergies:_____

Current medications: _____

General health: Good_____ Fair_____ Poor_____

Serious illnesses (dates): _____

_____

Do you smoke cigarettes? Y/N If so, how many packs per week? _____

What is your smoking history (i.e., yrs/amt) _____

Primary physician: _____ Work phone: (___)___-_____

Dance Training

List age when you started training and the specific technique(s):

_____

_____

Dance schools: _____

Age on pointe: _____ Where did you last train? _____

List age and length of time off from training ($\geq$ 2 mos): _____

Reason for time off: _____

Work Status: Student, apprentice, corps, soloist, principal, freelance dancer,
unemployed

Injury History (Nonsurgical)

Date	Body Part	Diagnosis	Time to Full Recovery
1			
2			
3			
4			
5			

Surgical Procedures (and Any Complications)

Date	Body Part	Diagnosis	Time to Full Recovery
1			
2			
3			
4			
5			

Conditioning Activities (e.g., Dance Class, Pilates, Swimming, Weights)

List specific types of exercises and frequency per week during four periods:

Breaks _____

Dance training _____

Rehearsals _____

Performances _____

Eating Behavior

Describe meals and snacks that you typically eat on a daily basis. _____

_____

Describe the typical amount of water, sodas, etc., that you drink daily. _____

_____

List any dietary restrictions (e.g., vegetarian). _____

_____

List daily intake of vitamins and supplements. _____

_____

Have you now, or in the past, had problems maintaining your optimal weight? If so, please explain. _____

_____

Menstrual History

Age of menarche (first period):_____

Have you ever had amenorrhea (no periods >3 months)? If so, at what age and for how long? _____

When was your last period? _____

Are you currently taking birth control pills? Y/N

Any Questions and/or Comments

_____
_____
_____
_____
_____
_____
_____
_____
_____
_____
_____
_____
_____
_____
_____
_____
_____
_____
_____
_____
_____
_____
_____
_____
_____
_____
_____
_____
_____
_____

Orthopedic Screening Form*

LEG LENGTH: Equal/Unequal   SCOLIOSIS: Mild/Moderate/Severe

   PALMS TO FLOOR: Y/N

AXIAL ALIGNMENT: Bowed/Knock-kneed/Pseudo-bowed/Straight

FIRST POSITION (GRAND PLIÉ):   Good/Fair/Poor   Asymmetrical Y/N   Pronation Y/N

SECOND POSITION (RELEVÉ):   Good/Fair/Poor   Asymmetrical Y/N   Sickling Y/N

FIFTH POSITION (ABILITY TO CLOSE):   Right: Good/Fair/Poor   Left: Good/Fair/Poor

SAUTÉ (3 TIMES):   Right: Roll-In   Strong/Weak   Soft/Hard
   Left: Roll-In   Strong/Weak   Soft/Hard

LUMBOSACRAL STEP-OFF (SPONDYLOLISTHESIS):   Y/N

HIP MOTION (PRONE):   Right: Good/Fair/Poor   Asymmetrical Y/N
   Left: Good/Fair/Poor

TURNOUT BELOW KNEE: Right: Good/Fair/Poor   Asymmetrical Y/N
   Left: Good/Fair/Poor

QUADRICEPS TIGHTNESS: Right/Left   HAMSTRING TIGHTNESS: Right/Left

HIP FLEXION/ADDUCTION SIGN (LABRAL TEAR):   Right/Left

PATELLAR MALALIGNMENT: Right/Left   PATELLAR TENDONITIS: Right/Left

ANKLE PLANTAR FLEXION: Right: Good/Fair/Poor   Asymmetrical Y/N
   Left: Good/Fair/Poor

PLANTAR FLEXION SIGN: Right/Left   DECREASED SUBTALAR MOTION: Right/Left

DRAWER SIGN: Right/Left   PERONEAL WEAKNESS: Right/Left   BUNION: Right/Left

FOOT TYPE: Peasant/Grecian/Egyptian/Model/Simian   ARCH: High/Normal/Low

Recommendations to the Physical Therapist:

_____

_____

_____

_____

_____

_____

_____

* Reprinted with permission. L. H. Hamilton, W. G. Hamilton, M.P. Warren, et al. "Factors Contributing to the Attrition Rate in Elite Ballet Students." *Journal of Dance Medicine & Science*, 1 (1997): 131–138.

Physical Fitness Screening*

Physical therapist Marika Molnar and chiropractor Lawrence De-Mann, Jr., designed this exam, using standard fitness tests adapted with dancers in mind. Its main purpose is to assess cardiovascular conditioning, imbalances within different muscle groups, asymmetries between the right and left sides, and flexibility. It should be performed by a dance medicine professional.

Cardiovascular Fitness

A fit heart should return to baseline, or resting heart rate, within one to three minutes after a vigorous workout. The practitioner takes your resting heart rate, then asks you to jump rope two-footed at your own pace for four minutes. Your heart rate is taken immediately afterward—usually within fifteen seconds after stopping the exercise. This step is repeated one minute later, at which point a fit dancer's pulse will have dropped by at least twenty beats. If this has not occurred, your pulse is taken three minutes later. Dancers whose pulse has not returned to its resting rate require an aerobic fitness program three times per week that suits their body type.

*Adapted from F. P. Kendall, E. K. McCreary, and P. G. Provance. *Muscle Testing and Function with Posture and Pain,* 4th ed. (Philadelphia, PA: Lippincott Williams & Wilkins, 1993).

Physical Strength

Your entire body needs to be strong to exercise and perform dance steps. To address this need, a fitness screening will evaluate strength in your lower extremities, trunk, and upper body.

For your lower-body test, you will stand on one leg in the neutral position (i.e., where the foot falls naturally while walking) with your arms held out to the side. The other leg is bent at the knee with the foot off the ground. A strong dancer should be able to do *twenty-five slow relevés* on each leg lightly holding on to something, rising steadily from flat foot to half-pointe with no demi-plié in between. Shaking or unevenness is a sign of weakness in the leg and ankle.

Peroneal strength in the two tendons running down the outside of the leg below the knee is necessary to prevent ankle sprains. Similar to the test in the orthopedic screening, you should be able to hold the pointed foot off the ground lying on the side in the winged position, resisting the practitioner's attempts to force each ankle out of this position.

Strong *hip flexors* are crucial for lifting the leg forward, whether to merely walk up a step or do a grand battement. Lying on your back with straight legs, raise one leg at a time in the turned-out position upward at a forty-five-degree angle (slightly to the side). The practitioner pushes down and outward to test the strength of the psoas muscle and the other extensors (the rectus and sartorius muscles). A strong dancer should be able to resist.

In contrast, *hip extensors* (buttocks, gluteals, and hamstrings) move the leg backward. Take the same position as above but with the knees bent ninety degrees and your pelvis raised to bring your back in line with the knees, like a bridge. Straighten one leg forward until it is level with the other knee and hold it on your own for 90 to 120 seconds. Anything less means the hip extensors are weak. This test is then repeated with the opposite leg. Asymmetries in strength between front and back hip muscles or right and left sides need to be corrected by exercise.

The trunk exam tests the abdominals in front and the extensors in the back. As the main core muscles of the body, the abdominals provide stability for almost every movement. These muscles include the lower, upper, and obliques (which cross over your abdomen like an *X*).

First, the *upper abdominal muscles* are tested. You lie on your back with your arms across your chest and hands on opposite shoulders. Sit up halfway with your legs straight. Hold this position against resistance, while the practitioner tries to push you down. The *oblique muscles* are tested in the same way, but instead of sitting up straight, you will twist to the opposite side. The practitioner pushes on your shoulders to see if he can break the position. Repeat on the other side. The final abdominal test involves the *lower abdominals*. This time, you will lie on your back and hold your legs up at a forty-five-degree angle. The practitioner stabilizes your trunk with one hand across your chest to keep you from rising up, while he pushes down against your legs with the other hand to try to break the position. Sufficient strength in each area is necessary to resist all three tests. If you can't, then remedial exercises are needed.

The last test that assesses strength in your lower body involves the *back extensor* muscles, which are necessary for good posture and partnering. Lie on your stomach and bend over the edge of the table at the waist, with your arms resting on your back. Raise your back until it is parallel to the table and maintain this position on your own for two minutes. An elite dancer is considered out of shape if he or she lets go at ninety seconds or less.

Our final series of tests measures the upper-body strength needed for partnering and arm movements. The first of these involves doing twenty-five *push-ups*. Men should do at least this amount in the standard way with straight legs; adult women should be able to do twenty-five with the knees on the floor.

The following tests of arm and shoulder include:

- The *deltoid* test, where you put your arms out sideways parallel to the floor in the standing position and hold them against resistance. If both arms give way, this signifies weakness. However, when only one arm goes down (while the other does not), this may be a sign of a rotator cuff injury in the weak shoulder.

- Testing the *supraspinatus* muscles, which lie on the upper border of the shoulder blades, is another way to assess the function of the rotator cuff. Hold your arms down at your sides and try to move them outward from the body against resistance. Weakness may indicate an injured rotator cuff in the shoulder.

- The *serratus* is one of the muscles under the armpits that helps to stabilize the shoulder blade. If this muscle is weak, one or both shoulder blades will stick out, or "wing." You can test this by raising your arms straight forward while resisting the practitioner's efforts to push them down.

- The main muscle for supporting and lifting the shoulders upward is the *trapezius,* which is divided into the upper, middle, and lower sections. You test the upper trapezius by trying to shrug your shoulders against resistance. To test the middle and lower trapezius, lie on your stomach with your hands in the small of your back forming a triangle with thumbs up. You will try to lift your arms against the practitioner pushing them down.

- The *rhomboid* is a back muscle that helps stabilize the shoulder blade. You can assess its strength by holding your arms behind and away from the back with the palms of the hand facing outward. If you can hold them in this position against resistance, you are strong in this area.

- A broad back muscle that also stabilizes the shoulder blade is the *latissimus dorsi*. Stand with your arms at your sides, internally rotated (turned in) so that the backs of your hands are touching the thighs. This position is held against resistance as the practitioner tries to pull the arms outward from the side.

- The *pectoralis* muscle, which lies beneath the breast area, provides strength to the shoulder joint. Lie down and raise your arms straight up toward the ceiling. In this position, the arms are pushed down to the side against resistance.

- The *biceps* muscle in the front of the upper arm is used to flex the elbow. You can test the strength of the biceps by holding the elbow bent at ninety degrees in front and perpendicular to the floor while the practitioner tries to straighten it.

- The *triceps* lies in the back of the upper arm and is used to keep the elbow straight. It has the opposite function of the biceps muscle. You can test it by trying to hold the elbow bent at ninety degrees against a force trying to bend it.

Flexibility

Generalized flexibility is essential for dancers. Tightness is the dancer's great enemy because it is a common precursor to muscle pulls or strains. This part of the exam is designed to detect tightness so that preventive steps can be taken to minimize injuries.

- Tightness in the lower back or *lumbar spine* can be evaluated by your ability to place your palms to the floor with your knees straight while standing.

- *Hip and thigh* tightness is tested in two ways. Lying on your stomach, place the heel of the foot on the buttock to check for tightness of the quadriceps muscle in the front of the thigh. Lying on your back, lift your leg while keeping the knee straight. Ideally, the leg should go to a minimum of ninety degrees, preferably more.

- The main structure tested in the *calf* for tightness is the Achilles tendon and its associated muscles. This is done while sitting by holding the ankle inward and trying to bring it up flexed at a right angle. Do it first with the knee straight and then with the knee bent. This makes it possible to evaluate separately the two muscle groups that attach to the Achilles tendon.

- The *ankle* needs to have full motion in both the ankle joint itself and the joint beneath the ankle, the subtalar joint. Tightness is checked by comparing the range of motion in your right and left sides by moving the heel in and out in the sitting position. Loss of motion in these joints can result in problems such as recurrent ankle sprains.

Recommendations

If needed, the practitioner will give the dancer specific strengthening or stretching exercises, as well as an individualized training program to implement at the gym.

Fitness Screening Form

Cardiovascular

FOUR-MINUTE JUMP-ROPE TEST

Resting HR____   Immediate post HR____   1 min post HR____   3 min post HR____

Strength (circle if weak)

1. LOWER BODY

   One leg relevé 25x   Right/Left

   Peroneals   Right/Left

   Hip Flexors   Right/Left

   Hip Extensors/Pelvic Raise ____30 ____60 ____90 ____120 Sec.

2. TRUNK

   Abdominals   Upper/Oblique/Lower

   Back Extensors ____30 ____60 ____90 ____120 Sec.

3. UPPER BODY

   Push-ups   M____   F____

   (circle if weak) Deltoid, Supraspinatus, Serratus, Trapezius, Rhomboid, Latissimus, Pectoralis, Biceps, Triceps

Flexibility (circle if tight)

Lumbar Region, Hips, Thigh, Calf, Ankle

Recommendations

_____
_____
_____
_____
_____
_____
_____

Hypermobility Screening*

Dancers who are born with benign joint hypermobility syndrome (BJHS) often have unstable joints, as well as minor symptoms, such as loose, stretchy skin. Dance training can accentuate hypermobility in the knee or ankle. In either case, a hypermobile joint is prone to injury because of instability, poor coordination, and inadequate proprioception. It is also a risk factor in osteoarthritis. The revised Brighton method of diagnosing BJHS by a health-care practitioner is based on both major and minor criteria, excluding similar genetic problems like Marfan or Ehlers-Danlos syndromes.

Requirement for Diagnosis (Any of the Following)

- Two major criteria

- One major plus two minor criteria

- Four minor criteria

- Two minor criteria and a clearly affected first-degree family member

There are two major criteria: (1) a past or current Beighton score ≥ 4; (2) or the presence of arthralgia (joint pain) in four or more joints for longer than three months. To get a Beighton score, two points are given to each of the first four questions (one point

*R. Grahame et al. "The Revised (Brighton 1998) Criteria for the Diagnosis of Benign Joint Hypermobility Syndrome (BJHS)." *Journal of Rheumatology* 27, no. 7 (2000): 1777–1779.

each for left and right sides) and one point for the fifth question for a total of nine possible points.

1. Can you push your thumb to your forearm?

2. Can you bend your little finger back ≥90 degrees?

3. Do your elbows bend back ≥10 degrees?

4. Do your knees hyperextend ≥10 degrees?

5. Can you touch your palms to the floor with straight legs?

The minor criteria are:

- Beighton score of 1, 2, or 3 (or 0–3 if fifty years of age or older)

- Pain, lasting more than three months, in one to three joints or in the back, spondylolysis, or spondylolisthesis

- Dislocation or subluxation in more than one joint, or in one joint more than one time

- Three or more soft tissue lesions (e.g., tennis elbow, tendonitis, inflamed bursa)

- Marfanoid habitus (i.e., tall, slim body shape with span-height ratio greater than 1.03; upper-lower segment ratio less than .89; long, skinny fingers)

- Skin: stretch marks, hyperelastic or thin skin, paper-thin scarring

- Eyes: drooping eyelids, myopia (nearsightedness), or down-slanted eyes

- Hernia, varicose veins, or rectal or uterine prolapse (bulging)

If you have benign joint hypermobility syndrome, your physical therapist will put you on a regular exercise program to help stabilize your joints. It is also advisable to avoid "popping," cracking, or over-stretching hypermobile joints.

Injury Reentry Form

Name: _____   Date of injury: _____

Injury diagnosis: _____

Treatment: no activity (days) _____   Physical therapy: Y/N

Surgery: Y/N   (Date: _____)

Current status: rehab program: Y/N

Weekly dance warm-up: Y/N   Weekly dance class: Y/N

Special Considerations

(e.g., dancer can do technique class but is not ready to jump)

_____

_____

_____

_____

_____

_____

_____   _____

Signature of physician/physical therapist   Date

_____

Signature of dancer

NOTE: It is the dancer's responsibility to: (1) have their health-care provider update this form as soon as their condition allows them to resume class, rehearsals, or perform-ances, and (2) ensure that artistic staff has a current record of their injury status.

The Dancer's Kitchen

Setting up a kitchen is an individual process. Each person has his or her own food preferences. Feel free to pick and choose from the following lists. Remember, this is bare bones. If you want to get serious, check out more extensive options for your kitchen in classic cookbooks like *The Joy of Cooking*. Bon appétit!

Things to Cook In

- An open jar or container on the kitchen counter to hold commonly used tools like wooden spoons and spatulas

- The best affordable aluminum or stainless-steel pots:

    One 4-quart aluminum pot with lid for pasta or soups and stews

    Three saucepans with lids: 1½-quart, 2-quart, 3-quart

- 12-inch and 8-inch (preferably iron) skillets with lids; Teflon damages easily and does not last

- Two sturdy pot holders

- Salt and pepper shakers

- Electric coffeemaker

- Toaster oven

- Microwave (if it fits within your budget)

Things to Cook With

- Knives: 3-inch paring, 6-inch utility (carbon stays sharper than stainless steel)

- A pair of tongs

- Vegetable peeler

- Metal measuring spoons

- Pyrex (heat-proof glass) measuring cups: one 4-cup size

- Wooden spoons

- Inexpensive cooking utensil set: long-handled fork, spoon, and spatula

- Wire whisk

- Strainer/sieve/colander to drain pasta or wash salads

- A French steamer insert (to place in pot to steam vegetables)

- 10-inch by 12-inch wooden chopping board

- Bottle and can openers

Optional Items

Rubber spatula, cheese grater, garlic press, spatter shield, Crock-Pot, electric skillet

In the Pantry

- Plastic wrap, aluminum foil, paper towels

- Iodized salt, black pepper

- Oregano, garlic, parsley flakes, paprika, cinnamon, ginger

- Raw nuts, natural peanut butter

- Mustard, ketchup

- Extra-virgin olive oil, cooking spray using canola oil

- Balsamic vinegar

- Low-sodium soy sauce

- Honey, sugar (to use sparingly)

- Canned crushed tomatoes

- Canned fruits (natural juice)

- Canned chunk light tuna in spring water (albacore tuna is higher in mercury)

- Whole-wheat pasta, brown rice

- Dried fruit, trail mix, protein bars

- Canned and dried beans

- Whole-grain cereal (oatmeal, etc.)

In the Refrigerator

Check expiration date on milk, eggs, and yogurt.

- 1 percent milk

- Butter substitute (no trans fat)

- Eggs

- Low-fat yogurt (plain)

- Low-fat cheese

- Low-fat mayonnaise

- Precut salads

- Fresh fruits

- Fresh vegetables

- Low-fat cottage cheese

In the Freezer

- Ice cubes

- Frozen vegetables

- Frozen veggie burgers

- Low-fat ice cream

- Frozen dinners (Amy's & Weight Watchers with less than 500 calories and 300 mg sodium)

- Whole-grain breads

- Whole-grain waffles

Cleanup and Kitchen Maintenance

- Small plastic dishpan, dish-washing detergent, and long-handle stiff bristle brush

- Plastic dish drainer; dishes will dry themselves

- Six cloth towels; more economical and environmentally friendly than paper towels

- Tough six-gallon plastic garbage can with lid that clamps shut

- Trash bags

Recommended Cookbooks

- Rachael Ray. *Rachael Ray Express Lane Meals: What to Keep on Hand, What to Buy Fresh for the Easiest-Ever 30-Minute Meals.* New York: Clarkson Potter, 2006.

- Deborah Madison. *Vegetarian Cooking for Everyone.* New York: Broadway, 1997.

- Irma Rombauer and Marion Rombauer Becker. *The Joy of Cooking.* New York: Scribner, 2006.

- Joy Bauer and Rosemary Black. *The 90/10 Weight Loss Cookbook.* New York: St. Martin's Griffin, 2005.

Food Diary Worksheet

KEEPING TABS OF CALORIES AND FAT IS OPTIONAL

Date: _____

TIME	FOOD/LIQUID	FEELINGS	CALORIES/FAT (grams)
____	_____	_____	_____
____	_____	_____	_____
____	_____	_____	_____
____	_____	_____	_____
____	_____	_____	_____
____	_____	_____	_____
____	_____	_____	_____
____	_____	_____	_____
____	_____	_____	_____
____	_____	_____	_____
____	_____	_____	_____
____	_____	_____	_____
____	_____	_____	_____
____	_____	_____	_____
____	_____	_____	_____
____	_____	_____	_____
____	_____	_____	_____
____	_____	_____	_____
____	_____	_____	_____

Total: _____

Stress Diary Worksheet

Date: _____

STRESSFUL SITUATION	AUTOMATIC THOUGHT IMAGE	RATIONAL RESPONSE
Describe the event that led to an uncomfortable emotion.	Note your automatic thought or image that preceded the emotion.	Write a rational response to counter the automatic thought/image. (Note: You need to believe it.)

Bibliography

American Psychiatric Association. *Diagnostic and Statistical Manual of Mental Disorders,* 4th edition, text revision. Washington, D.C., American Psychiatric Association, 2000.

Behm, D. G., Bambury, A., Cahill, F., and Power, K. "Effect of Acute Static Stretching on Force, Balance, Reaction Time, and Movement Time." *Medicine & Science in Sports & Exercise* 36 (2004): 1397–1402.

Bennett, W., and Gurin, J. *The Dieter's Dilemma: Why Diets Are Obsolete. The New Setpoint Theory of Weight Control.* New York: Basic Books, 1982.

Bodger, C. *Smart Guide to Relieving Stress.* New York: John Wiley & Sons, 1999.

Bronner, S., and Worthen, L. "The Demographics of Dance in the United States." *Journal of Dance Medicine & Science* 3 (1999): 151–153.

Carroll, L. "Scientists Discover 'Skinny' Gene." *Fitness,* MSNBC.com, 2007, pp. 1–5.

Centers for Disease Control and Prevention. *Physical Activity and Health: A Report of the Surgeon General.* Atlanta, GA: U.S. Department of Health and Human Services, 1996.

Clippinger, K. "Supplemental Strength Training for Young Dancers." *Journal of Dance Medicine & Science* 2 (1998): 75–76.

Deighan, M. A. "Flexibility in Dance." *Journal of Dance Medicine & Science* 9 (2005): 13–17.

Fitzpatrick, L., and Heaney, R. P. "Got Soda?" *Journal of Bone and Mineral Research* 18 (2003): 1570–1572.

Flett, G. L., and Hewitt, P. L. "Perfectionism and Maladjustment: An Overview of Theoretical, Definitional, and Treatment Issues," in G. L. Flett and P. L. Hewitt (eds.), *Perfectionism: Theory, Research, and Treatment.* Washington, D.C.: American Psychological Association, 2002.

Grahame, R., et al. "The Revised (Brighton 1998) Criteria for the Diagnosis of Benign Joint Hypermobility Syndrome (BJHS)." *Journal of Rheumatology* 27, no. 7 (2000): 1777–1779.

Hamilton, L. H. *The Person Behind the Mask: A Guide to Performing Arts Psychology.* Westport, CT: Greenwood Publishers, 1997.

———. "A Psychological Approach to the Rehabilitation of Injured Performers." *Orthopaedic Physical Therapy Clinics of North America* 6 (1997): 131–143.

———. *Advice for Dancers: Emotional Counsel and Practical Strategies.* San Francisco: Jossey-Bass Publishers, 1998.

———. "A Psychological Profile of the Adolescent Dancer." *Journal of Dance Medicine & Science* 3 (1999): 48–50.

———. "Helping Dancers Eat Right and Stay Fit." *Choreography and Dance* 6 (2001): 31–37.

———. "Ouch! Five Common Dance Injuries and How to Treat Them." *Dance Magazine* (April 2005): 65–71.

———, Hamilton, W. G., and Marshall, P. "Risk Factors Associated with Physical Disability Among Injured Dancers." Paper presented at the 113th Annual Convention of the American Psychological Association, Washington, D.C., August 2005.

———, Hamilton, W. G., Warren, M. P., Keller, K., and Molnar, M. "Factors Contributing to the Attrition Rate in Elite Ballet Students." *Journal of Dance Medicine & Science* 1 (1997): 131–138.

———, Solomon, R., and Solomon, J. "A Proposal for Standardized Psychological Screening of Dancers." *Journal of Dance Medicine & Science* 10 (2006): 40–45.

Hamilton, W. G., Hamilton, L. H., Marshall, P., and Molnar, M. "A Profile of the Musculoskeletal Characteristics of Elite Professional Ballet Dancers." *American Journal of Sports Medicine* 20 (1992): 267–273.

Jennings, J., and Davies, G. J. "Treatment of Cuboid Syndrome Secondary to Lateral Ankle Sprains: A Case Series." *Journal of Orthopaedic and Sports Physical Therapy* 35 (2005): 409–415.

Kish, R. L., Plastino, J. G., and Martyn-Stevens, B. "A Young Dancer Survey." *Medical Problems of Performing Artists* 18 (2003): 161–165.

Korpelainen, R., Orava, S., Karpakka, J., Siira, P., and Hulkko, A. "Risk Factors for Recurrent Stress Fractures in Athletes." *American Journal of Sports Medicine* 29 (2001): 304–310.

Koutedakis, Y., Myszkewycz, L., Soulas, D., et al. "The Effects of Rest and Subsequent Training on Selected Physiological Parameters in Professional Female Classical Dancers." *International Journal of Sports Medicine* 20 (1999): 379–383.

Koutedakis, Y., Stavropoulos-Kalinoglou, A., and Metsios, G. "The Significance of Muscular Strength in Dance." *Journal of Dance Medicine & Science* 9 (2005): 29–34.

Laws, H. *Fit to Dance,* vol. 2. London: Dance UK, 2005.

Liederbach, M., and Compagno, J. M. "Psychological Aspects of Fatigue-Related Injuries in Dancers." *Journal of Dance Medicine & Science* 5 (2001): 116–120.

Marshall, P., and Hamilton, W. G. "Cuboid Subluxation in Ballet Dancers." *American Journal of Sports Medicine* 20 (1992): 169–175.

Molnar, M. *Fundamentals II. Exercise Directives for Fitness Professionals.* Sante Fe, NM: Physicalmind Institute, 1997.

Mozaffarian, D., Katan, M. B., Ascherio, A., et al. "Trans Fatty Acids and Cardiovascular Disease." *New England Journal of Medicine* 354 (2006): 1601–1613.

Nicholas, J. A. "Risk Factors, Sports Medicine and the Orthopedic System: An Overview." *Journal of Sports Medicine* 3 (1975): 243–259.

Prochaska, J. O., Norcross, J. C., and DiClemente, C. C. *Changing for Good*. New York: HarperCollins, 1994.

———, Norcross, J. C., and DiClemente, C. C. "Stages of Change: Prescriptive Guidelines," in G. P. Koocher and J. C. Norcross (eds.), *Psychologists' Desk Reference,* 2nd edition. New York: Oxford University Press, 2005.

Purnell, M., Shirley, D., and Crookshanks, D. "Risk Factors Associated with Adolescent Dance Injuries." *Proceedings of the 13th Annual Meeting of the International Association for Dance Medicine & Science.* (October 2003): 99–101.

Rovere, G. D., Webb, L. X., Gristina, A. G., and Vogel, J. M. "Musculoskeletal Injuries in Theatrical Dance Students." *American Journal of Sports Medicine* 11 (1983): 195–198.

Selye, H. *The Stress of Life.* London: Longmans, Green, 1950.

Shrier, I., and Gossal, K. "Myths and Truths About Stretching. Individualized Recommendations for Healthy Muscles." *The Physician and Sportsmedicine* 28 (2000): 57–63.

Smith, L. L. "Cytokine Hypothesis of Overtraining: A Physiological Adaptation to Excessive Stress?" *Medicine & Science in Sports & Exercise* 32 (2000): 317–331.

Smith, R. E., Ptacek, J. T., and Patterson, E. "Moderator Effects of Cognitive and Somatic Trait Anxiety on the Relation Between Life Stress and Physical Injuries." *Anxiety, Stress, and Coping* 23 (2000): 269–288.

Stacey, J. M. "The Physiological Development of the Adolescent Dancer." *Journal of Dance Medicine & Science* 3 (1999): 59–65.

Stokes, K. A., Nevill, M. E., Hall, G. M., and Lakomy, H. K. "The Time Course of the Human Growth Hormone Response to a 60 S and 30 S Cycle Ergometer Sprint." *Journal of Sports Science* 20 (2002): 487–494.

Verma R. B., and Sherman, O. "Athletic Stress Fractures: Part 1. History, Epidemiology, Physiology, Risk Factors, Radiography, Diagnosis, and Treatment." *American Journal of Orthopedics* 25 (2001): 798–806.

Wansink, B. *Mindless Eating: Why We Eat More Than We Think.* New York: Bantam Books, 2006.

Whitney, E. N., and Rolfes, S. R. *Understanding Nutrition,* 9th ed. Belmont, CA: Wadsworth, 2002.

Wilkinson, M., and Williams, A. "Too Much of a Good Thing? Why Increased Joint Flexibility May Damage Your Distance Performance." *Peak Performance* 175 (2003): 5–6.

Winerman, L. "Sleep Deprivation Threatens Public Health, Says Research Award Winner." *Monitor on Psychology* (July/August 2004): 61.

Winner, E. *Gifted Children: Myths and Realities.* New York: Basic Books, 1996.

Wyon, M. "Cardiorespiratory Training for Dancers." *Journal of Dance Medicine & Science* 9 (2005): 7–12.

Index

Abergel, Dena, 83, 129
Access to Health Insurance/Resources
    for Care, 158
Actors Fund, 157
acupuncture, 28
Addiction Resource Guide, 160
The Addiction Workbook
    (Fanning/O'Neill), 160
adolescence
    body awareness during, 50–51
    shoe resizing during, 55
    stretching during, 78–79, 154
    weight lifting during, 154, 168
Advice for Dancers (Hamilton, L.), 115
aerobic conditioning, 31–32, 34
    endurance and, 73–74
    heart rate goals in, 75–76
    muscle modification and, 52–53
    negatives of, 74–75
    program examples for, 85–87
    weight management using, 118, 123,
    128
Agon, 144
Alcoholics Anonymous, 137, 160
Al Hirschfeld Free Health Clinic, 158
amenorrhea. *See* menstrual problems
American Academy of Orthopedic
    Surgeons, 28, 155
American College of Sports Medicine,
    97, 138
American Council on Exercise, 28, 156
American Dietetic Association, 28, 77, 90,
    129, 158
American Guild of Musical Artists, 38
American Harlequin Corporation, 18,
    154
American Massage Therapy Association,
    156

American Orthopedic Foot & Ankle
    Society, 155
American Physical Therapy Association,
    28, 155
American Psychiatric Association, 115
American Psychological Association, 28,
    137, 156
anorexia nervosa, 41, 114
    warning signs for, 115–16
    weight gain during treatment of, 119,
    122
arch, foot, 64
    ballet positions' relation to, 56, 173,
    179–80
aromatherapy, 149
arthritis, 59, 166
    osteo-, 32, 193
ArtistAccess, 157
asymmetry, structural/functional
    awareness of, xix, 7, 29–30, 51–52,
    171–72, 173
    pointe work and, 29–30, 51, 174,
    177–78
    turnout and, xix, 29–30, 34, 50, 166,
    173–75, 177
awareness, body, 11, 26
    during adolescence/developmental
    period, 50–51
    of asymmetry, structural/functional,
    xix, 7, 29–30, 51–52, 171–72, 173
    of flexibility, 31, 53–55, 172
    of foot/arch type, 55–56, 173,
    179–80
    injury avoidance via, 7–8, 21
    of muscular strength/endurance, 52–53
    of turnout, 29–30, 57–59, 166, 173–75,
    177
axial alignment, 173

211

stretching/range of motion, 9, 54–55,
61–63, 78–80, 80–84, 154
yoga, 17, 28, 55, 61, 82, 83, 123, 155
Cunningham, Merce, 60

dance. *See also* dancers
body types associated with, 113
eating before, during, after, 98–99
evolution of, xiii–xiv, 4
varieties of, 4–5
dance attire/equipment
as occupational hazard, 18–19
resources for, 153–54
Dance Magazine, xviii, 114, 137
dance medicine. *See* medical treatment
dancers. *See also* challenges, dancer; work
habits, healthy
challenges common to, 13–22
outside employment of, 28, 156
dancer's kitchen
cleanup/maintenance items in, 200
cookbook recommendations for,
200–201
cooking appliances in, 197
cooking utensils in, 198
freezer items in, 200
pantry items in, 198–99
refrigerated items in, 199–200
the Dancers' Resource (Actors Fund), 157
Dance Spirit (magazine), 154
Dance Teacher (magazine), 154
De Luz, Joaquin, *48,* 49, 122
DeMann, Lawrence, Jr., xiv, xvii, 8
asymmetry and, 51
physical fitness screenings and, 34, 185
strength training and, 78
diet, 9. *See also* eating disorders; lifestyle,
diet; weight management
before, during, after exercise, 98–99
bone loss related to, 120–22
caloric needs/counting in, 91, 103–9,
159
carbohydrates in, 92–93, 128
case studies highlighting, 103–9
counseling on, 8, 18, 32–33, 95, 116–17,
129
do's and don'ts for, 90–91
fat in, 95–96, 105, 108–9, 129–30
food diary analysis of, xix, 33, 44, 103,
105, 107, 109–11, 122, 203

food groups and, 92–96
food preparation and, 100–101
hydration in, 33, 68, 96–97, 98–99,
103–9, 158
injury rehabilitation via, 17–18, 21, 32,
90, 91, 94, 99
lifestyle habits' influence on, 107–9,
124–28, 131, 159
menstrual problems related to, 17, 91,
104–5, 116, 120–22, 128
nutritional labels/indexes and, 89, 90,
101
obstacles to healthy, 101–3
protein in, 21, 32, 94–95, 99, 128–29
resources for, 89, 90, 97, 98, 101, 104,
107, 156–57, 158–59
stress management via, 27, 39–45
supplements to, 97–98, 105, 107, 123,
149
dining out, 107–9, 127–28, 131, 159
Do It Now Foundation, 160
Dying to Be Thin (VHS/DVD), 156
dynamic stretching, 62. *See also* stretching

Eating Disorder Referral and
Information Center, 156–57
eating disorders, 33. *See also* diet; weight
management
anorexia nervosa, 41, 114, 115–16, 119,
122
bulimia nervosa, 116–17
resources for, 42–43, 156–57
Edge, Amanda, *48,* 49
education. *See* awareness, body
Emergency Fund for Student Dancers,
157
Entertainment Industry Group Insurance
Trust, 158
Étoile Polaire, 25
Evans, Albert, *36, 37, 132,* 133

fat in diet, 95–96, 105, 108–9, 129–30. *See
also* diet
Fayette, James, 38
feet
arches of, 56, 64, 173, 179–80
bunions on, 30–31, 165, 179
caring for, 55, 58
injuries to, 7–8, 18–19, 23, 75, 165
types of, 30, 55–56, 179

Feld, Eliot, 25
finances
    employment outside dance and, 28
    resources for, 28, 157–58
flexibility, 78–80. *See also* stretching
    factors in, 53
    hypermobility's relation to, 26, 54
    screenings for, 31, 172, 189–90
    tight muscles and, 54–55, 189–90
food diary(ies)
    case studies on, 103, 105, 107, 109–11
    weight management via, xix, 33, 44,
        109–11, 122
    worksheet, blank, 203
    worksheet, completed, 110
food preparation, 100–101. *See also*
        lifestyle, diet
The Four Temperaments (Balanchine), 144

gender
    dietary considerations related to,
        89–90, 102
    injury variances by, 17, 18, 23
    strength training and, 77–78
    water intake and, 33
    weight goals/management and, 32,
        118–19
George Balanchine Trust, 100
Gilliland, Kaitlyn, *24, 25*
Guiding Stars nutritional index, 101,
    158
Gyrotonic Expansion System, 61
    conditioning aspects of, 77, 80, 123
    principles of, 81–82
    resources for, 82, 155

Hamilton, William G., xiv, xvii, 8, 20
    injuries and, 54, 59
    orthopedic screenings and, 6–7, 34, 171
    periodization and, 66
Hannaford Brothers, 101, 158
Healthy Highways (Goldbeck/Goldbeck),
    159
Hendrickson, Adam, *12,* 13, 18
Horvath, Juliu, 81–82
hydration, 33, 96. *See also* diet
    before, during, after exercise, 98–99
    case studies on, 103–9
    enhanced drinks and, 106–7
    NSAID use and, 68

over-, 97
resources for, 158
hypermobility (loose joints), 21
    injury's relation to, 18, 19, 26, 54, 56,
        193
    resources for, 154
    stabilization exercises for, 31, 53
hypermobility screening, 8, 32
    BJHS diagnosis requirements in,
        193–94
    Hypermobility Syndrome Association,
        154

IADMS. *See* International Association for
        Dance Medicine & Science
inflammation, 9, 67–69, 163
injuries. *See also* medical treatment
    ankle, 19–20, 21, 29–30, 31, 53, 75,
        164–65, 178–79
    back, 4, 18, 75, 167, 175
    bunions as, 30–31, 165, 179
    calf, 21, 61, 165
    diet's role in overcoming, 17–18, 21,
        32, 90, 91, 94, 99
    elbow/wrist/hand, 165
    foot, 7–8, 18–19, 23, 75, 165
    gender's relation to, 17, 18, 23
    glossary of terms defining, 163–64
    hamstring, 4, 7, 30, 61, 79–80
    hip, 7, 30, 57–59, 75, 165–66, 176–77
    hypermobility's relation to, 18, 19, 26,
        54, 56, 193
    inflammation and, 67–69, 163
    knee, 14–15, 23, 25, 29, 31, 49, 54, 75,
        166–67, 173, 177
    minor, 67–69
    neck, 168
    NSAID use for, 68
    reentry forms post-, 68, 195
    resources for, 155–56
    RICE treatment for, 67
    shin, 168
    shoulder, 23, 168, 187–88
    sleep's relation to, 23, 69, 149
    stress management's relation to, 16, 20,
        23, 137–39
    survey statistics on, 23
    tendonitis, 7, 21, 29, 56, 59, 64, 72,
        164–66, 177
insurance, 157–58

Stafford, Abi, xix, *70*
  behavioral change and, 45
  cross-training/rehabilitation by, 31, 32,
    53, 66, 71, 75, 80, 82, 85
  diet's impact on, 89, 97
  injury by, 19–20, 53
  stress management by, 138
  warmups by, 60
  weight management by, 123
static stretching, 62. *See also* stretching
Stork position, 54
strength testing. *See* physical strength
    testing
strength training, 31. *See also specific*
    training categories
  via Gyrotonic, 61, 77, 80, 81–82, 123, 155
  muscle fiber modification via, 53
  via Pilates, 28, 34, 50–51, 53, 57, 61, 66,
    72, 77, 80–81, 85–86, 123, 155
  resources for, 78, 81, 82
  via weight lifting, 55, 77–78, 83–84,
    128
  via yoga, 17, 28, 55, 61, 82, 83, 123, 155
stress diary(ies), 146–47
  worksheet, blank, 205
  worksheet, completed, 148
stress management, xix, 9, 21, 26, 133
  breathing techniques for, 144–45, 159
  CBT for, 27, 44, 146–48
  coping skills for, 137
  diaries for, 146–48, 205
  diet and, 27, 39–45
  downtime/decompressing for, 148–50
  injury prevention and, 16, 20, 23,
    137–39
  journal-keeping for, 145–46
  meditation for, 145
  perfectionism's relation to, 136–37
  physical reactions to stress and, 139–41
  resources for, 27–28, 136, 137, 143, 144,
    159
  scenarios of stress and, 134–36
  sleep's role in, 27, 142–43, 149
  social support for, 27
  stages of stress and, 140–41
  warning signs of stress and, 134
  weight management and, 17
stretching, 9, 84
  in adolescence, 78–79, 154
  before and after activities, 61

cautions regarding, 54–55, 78–79
  resources for, 154
  selection of programs for, 80–83
  techniques, 62–63
  weakening of muscles from, 54–55
Stretching (Anderson), 80, 154
subluxation, 7, 54, 166, 168, 177, 194
substance use/abuse
  behavioral stages and, 41
  resources for, 43, 137, 160
supplements, dietary, 97–98, 105, 107
  overwork/stress and, 149
  weight loss and, 123
Swan Lake, 137

tendonitis, 7, 21
  Achilles, 64, 164
  asymmetry contributing to, 29, 56, 59
  iliopsoas, 165
  from overwork, 72, 165
  patellar, 166, 177
tests, medical, 20, 21, 30, 169–70
Tharp, Twyla, 74
Theme and Variations (Balanchine), 60
Theraband, 53
Tricks of the Trade (DVD), 154
turnout, 75
  asymmetry's relation to, xix, 29–30, 34,
    50, 166, 173–75, 177
  increases of, 57–59, 174

University of Chicago, 17
University of Minnesota School of
    Public Health, 120
University of Newfoundland, 79

Van Cauter, Eve, 17
Vegetarian Cooking for Everyone
    (Madison), 201

Walker, Elizabeth, *36,* 37, 102
  stress management by, 146
Wansink, Brian, 122, 124–27, 161
warming up, 9, 15, 59–61
Warren, Michelle, 97, 119, 121
water intake. *See* hydration
weight management, xix, 9. *See also*
    dancer's kitchen; diet; eating
    disorders
  behavioral case study on, 39–45

body ideals for dance and, 113
dieting negatives related to, 114–22
diet/nutrition counseling for, 8, 18,
  32–33, 95, 116–17, 129
food diaries for, xix, 33, 44, 109–11, 122
gender variances in, 32, 118–19
lifestyle factors influencing, 124–28,
  131
moderation as approach to, 128–29, 130
quick tips for, 131
resources for, 115, 117, 121, 123, 129,
  160–61
set points and, 118, 119, 123
stress's impact on, 17
weight gain and, 119–20, 122–23, 131
weight loss and, 120–22, 123–24,
  128–29, 131
weight training, 77–78. *See also* strength
  training
  gaining/losing weight via, 128
  muscle fiber modification via, 53
  recommendations for, 83–84
wellness. *See also specific categories*
  awareness/education's role in, xix, 7–8,
    11, 21, 26, 29–31, 50–59, 166,
    171–72, 173–75, 177, 179–80
  behavioral change stages and, 38–45
  holistic approach to, 25–35
  resources for mind-body, 7, 27–28,
    42–43, 55, 58, 75, 78, 81, 82, 89, 90,
    97, 98, 101, 104, 107, 115, 117, 121,
    123, 129, 136, 137, 143, 144, 153–61
  screenings for, xix, 8, 29–35, 50, 54,
    129, 171–83, 185–91, 193–94
  social support for, 27
  stress management for, xix, 9, 16–17,
    20–21, 23, 26–28, 39–45, 133–50,
    159, 205
  stumbling blocks to, 37–38
wellness program, NYCB, xviii, 3–4, 10
  approaches used by, 5–9

awareness/education as part of, 7–8,
  11, 21
health-care specialists within, xiv
highlights of survey by, 23
medical assistance within, 6–7
objectives of, 5
performance tips as part of, 8–9
screenings as part of, xix, 8, 29–35, 50,
  54, 129, 171–83, 185–91, 193–94
wellness awareness quiz in, 11
Whelan, Wendy, 68–69, 82
"When Can I Start Pointe Work?"
  (IADMS), 55, 154
whirlpools, 149
Woetzel, Damian, *48,* 49
Workers' Compensation, 158
  claims for, 5–6
work habits, healthy, xix, 9, 49. *See also*
  wellness; *specific work habits*
  awareness of body as, xix, 7–8, 11, 21,
    26, 29–31, 50–59, 166, 171–72,
    173–75, 177, 179–80
  cooling down as, 9, 63–64
  inflammation/pain treatment as, 9,
    67–69
  periodization as, 9, 14–15, 16, 23,
    65–67, 72, 85–87
  stretching as, 9, 54–55, 61–63, 78–80,
    80–84, 154
  warming up as, 9, 15, 59–61
World Wide Online Meditation Center,
  159
Wyon, Mathew, 77

yoga, 17, 28, 82, 123
  "hot," 55
  principles of, 83
  resources for, 155
  warmups using, 61
Yoga Alliance, 155
Yoga for Dancers, 83, 155

Abi Stafford

NEW
YORK
CITY
BALLET

nycballet.com